WHAT IF?

WHAT IF?

TWENTY-TWO SCENARIOS IN SEARCH OF IMAGES

VILÉM FLUSSER

TRANSLATED BY ANKE FINGER AND

KENNETH KRONENBERG

University of Minnesota Press

Minneapolis

London

The University of Minnesota Press gratefully acknowledges the financial assistance provided for the publication of this book by Greenhouse Studios at the University of Connecticut, through a grant from The Andrew W. Mellon Foundation.

Published by the University of Minnesota Press
111 Third Avenue South, Suite 290
Minneapolis, MN 55401-2520
http://www.upress.umn.edu

ISBN 978-1-5179-1365-6 (hc)
ISBN 978-1-5179-1366-3 (pb)

A Cataloging-in-Publication record for this book is available from the Library of Congress.

Available as a Manifold edition at manifold.umn.edu

Printed in the United States of America on acid-free paper

The University of Minnesota is an equal-opportunity educator and employer.

31 30 29 28 27 26 25 24 23 22   10 9 8 7 6 5 4 3 2 1

Wanted: all those whose imagination enables them to recode into video images the ideas and concepts presented in this series of scenarios. We invite all who are able to program these images in some way or other to get in touch with European Photography by telephone or in writing . . .

To my cousin David Flusser, who in good Judeo-Christian fashion, always assumes the best.

CONTENTS

INTRODUCTION

Into the Slipstream of Flusser's "Field of Possibilities"

ANKE FINGER

In 1988, Vilém Flusser (1920–91) is invited to address the TV Club of Vienna with a lecture on "Science Fiction." He defines science fiction as a "grey zone within which science and fiction (fact and fiction) overlap," but he generally considers this area of literary production "a disappointment": "We expect texts that establish fictitious scientific hypotheses and then, forthcoming as a result, fictitious theories, for example, imagined alternatives to Darwin or Einstein. Regrettably, we have to discover that the imagination is more alive in the works of hard science than in most science fiction texts, by far." At issue, according to Flusser, is the contemporary concept of truth. To move beyond what he observes as a paralyzing binary, we must unlearn the habit to seek clear differences between "right" and "wrong", between "true" and "untrue." He proposes to revivify scholastic and Talmudic traditions by aiming for "a level of the absurd" such that "truth will somehow shine through." In short, we should start to consider science fiction as an epistemology of the weird, a "counter science" to the hard sciences that demands of the author a "simultaneous zest for the improbable and scientific rigor."[1] A year later, he publishes *Angenommen: Eine Szenenfolge,* and the Berlin Wall comes down.

That same year, far, far away, Bruce Sterling, too, laments that "Science Fiction—much like the former Vanguard of Progressive Mankind, the Communist Party—has lost touch with its cultural reasons for being." Accusing especially "hard" science fiction of having lost its "inner identity," devoid of innovation and creativity, Sterling sets out to coin a new genre by describing what he perceives as a "contemporary kind of writing which has set its face against consensus reality. It is fantastic, surreal at times, speculative on occasion, but not rigorously so.... This is a kind of writing which makes you feel very strange.... We would call this kind of fiction Novels of Postmodern Sensibility, but that looks pretty bad on a category rack [. . .]; so for the sake of convenience and argument, we will call these books 'slipstream.'"[2]

What If?, now the English translation of *Angenommen* and one of Vilém Flusser's last books, has endured something of an outsider status among the vast oeuvre he has produced over forty years and in more than four languages. While the last two decades have brought forth a plethora of new editions, as well as scholarship, exhibitions, and conferences on the substantial volume and network of Flusser's writings and ideas, *What If?* has remained sidelined—not entirely "at home" either in his media philosophy, or in what has been called his "scientific writing" or "philosophical fiction," as his friend Abraham Moles called it, or in his writings on design, on language and communication, on history, and so forth. It simply does not seem to fit, really, into any of the categories now more or less established in Flusser scholarship. To this day, little has been said about this text at all. If anything, it is handled as a film or television script—including by myself in the introduction to *Vilém Flusser: An Introduction* (2011), where I referred to the structure of twenty-two scenarios as "vignettes"—unsure how to assign a thematic arch, a narrative coherence, a contemporary or current locus.[3] This set of micro-essays Flusser refers to, in the first scenario, as "a series motivated by curiosity," an "unreasonable endeavor" and "an invitation to an impossible journey," appears to be a kind of hopscotch of ramblings and musings. Defying "reason" and embarking on an "impossible" trip may entice at the outset, but what, in fact, is the reader to make of meeting an intellectually (and sexually) poised tapeworm ready to become a model for humanity, the biblical Abraham cloaked as a modern-day cranky and avuncular misanthrope, a brand-new paragraph-eating insect categorized as *Bibliophagus convictus*, a political party from the twenty-third century, a scientist who promotes creativity by means of population control, a genetically modified Zebu cow called "Super-Kali," catastrophes hailed as productive, and Shamans, Jesus, and Martin Heidegger all in one place?

The twenty-two fictitious micro-essays Vilém Flusser termed "scenarios of the future" are organized into three sets of different life-worlds, entitled "Scenes from Family Life," "Scenes from Economic Life," and "Scenes from Politics." The author explicitly implores readers at the outset ("Wanted!"), in a dedication of the book to his cousin, David Flusser, to dare to transcode the written scenarios into images, that is, to turn the text into a film or a set of videos—in 1989, the new media of the time. According to Gustavo Bernardo, the "philosophical poet and poetical philosopher . . . is searching for a style of writing and thinking that can express his speculative position with the goal to develop and stimulate new ideas."[4] New ideas, to Flusser, are generated by (technical) images, by code. While the universe Flusser created with his previous book, *Vampyroteuthis Infernalis*, explores a single alternate lifeworld coherent in its mirroring of the human species by a cephalopod, each scenario in *What If?* suggests a variety of new ideas, given the speculative, projecting nature of their setting—in the best and most creative sense of "what if"—in the past, the present, or the future. They range from the scientific to the fantastic, to the outrageous and provocative, and certainly include the playful and whimsical. As such, *What If?*, the TV series—these days, an obligatory three seasons, following the text's structure, with 6–7 episodes each—could be entertaining and reflective, thought-provoking, exasperating, stimulating, constructive, and decidedly off-kilter. A campy *Black Mirror*, perhaps.

What If?: The Past

In 1989, nothing came of the plans to create images from the text. Few comment on the genealogy of the manuscript, fewer write about

What If? at all. Most prominent among them is the Swiss author Felix
Phillip Ingold, a good friend of Flusser's and a frequent correspondent.
As Daniel Irrgang has documented in his important discussion of the
almost decade-long exchange of letters, Flusser, upon finishing his
manuscript of *Vampyroteuthis Infernalis* in 1981, contemplated
intensely the "difference between Science fiction and Fictitious science . . . , in short: what's the difference between hypotheses and
fables?"[5] According to Irrgang, the first scenario, a so-called "pre-text,"
for *What If?*, reached Ingold in the fall of 1987, and while Ingold
attempted to interest the Genevan station Télévision Remande in the
project, he himself was skeptical whether Flusser's goal of encoding
the text into images was feasible. Flusser, in turn, tried to further
explicate his idea of the technical image, but Ingold, unflappable, and
with a precise sense of the slippage in Flusser's vision, detected an
"unsolvable issue: namely the fact that you are writing far beyond
concepts only [since] you render effective the knowledge packed into a
concept within the context of scenes, which you flesh out with great
powers of the imagination only to declare thereafter, in case of a possible TV-production, that merely the concepts are to be put into
images."[6] While their correspondence ended in 1990, Ingold remained
fascinated by this small piece of science fiction his friend shared with
him shortly before his untimely death. Twenty-eight years later, in a
lengthy article honoring Vilém Flusser published in the *Neue Zürcher
Zeitung,* Ingold offers his own reading of Flusser's oeuvre, emphasizing
Flusser's revolt against academic conventions, his insistence, obses-
sion even, on writing as a "permanent learning curve," and describing
his output, articles, op-eds, stories, anecdotes, scenes, letters, essayistic texts, as invitations for nomadic reading, a nonlinear pursuit akin
to scanning or screen-hopping. Ingold explicitly singles out *What If?*,
applauding Flusser's uncanny foresight, especially with scenario seventeen, "Perpetual Peace"—a nod to Immanuel Kant's famous treatise
of the same name from 1795: "Flusser foresaw, already back then, in
the late 1980s, a period of rapid stagnancy, a global standstill, unpleas-
antly completing the promise of 'perpetual peace.'"[7] History is
composed and computed, it is being made, including by "potentates
such as Trump, Putin, Xi Jinping"; engaged as "makers (fakers) of

history, they show themselves to act as handlers and artists, as deceptive geniuses and theurgists." Ingold concludes his commemoration by describing Flusser as a "sharp-sighted and distinctly headstrong apocalyptic thinker."[8]

Beyond Ingold's involvement in the composition of *What If?*, and his recall of a text he deems possibly more compelling today, thirty years later, than in 1989, the literature is thin. Petra Gropp, in her erudite and detailed discussion of Flusser in *Szenen der Schrift* (2006) grants the book a short paragraph, reading it as a "hybrid text, oriented towards the techno-imaginary," with scenes playing to "traditional, literary forms of travel and adventure literature."[9] Heiko Christians, delineating the conceptual history of "scenario" by pointing to Hermann Kahn, Stanley Kubrick's template for *Dr. Strangelove*, and Anthony J. Wiener, makes us aware that Flusser employed the scenario technique not to play with the "futurist" implications of a scenario versus a scene.[10] Rather, as specified in the first scenario, he sought to "integrate the factor of a finite existence, removed from media, and the dialog format as a scenic base structure of communication, he crossed futurology, cybernetics and dialogic existentialism all in one."[11] According to Christians, as Flusser points to death as part of the field of possibilities, he embraces the anthropology of this endeavor: the human is an animal that feeds on improbabilities—naturally, the scenarios will provide precisely that. Flusser himself underscores the scenarios' virtualities in one of his last lectures from 1991:

> We are in the same situation as a magnet. . . . Everything around us approaches from all directions and all times. . . . Linguistic thought is bankrupt. Everything comes close. Lines are no more. Progress, regress, all of that is pointless. It comes closer. It approaches, not unendingly, but not exactly in chaos, either. There is this tendency towards becoming-more-probable that is contradicted by tendencies towards becoming-more-improbable. Virtualities intersect, and because they intersect accidentally, they become even more virtual. Some prevail. One is almost here. At the last moment, it disappears. I don't know if I was able to describe this dramatically enough."[12]

What If?: The Present

Perhaps readers and scholars have all been looking in the wrong place, working with unworkable categories to place *What If?* into literary or philosophical contexts and bookshelves that turned out to be not only unaccommodating but possibly hostile to its contents. Let me suggest that the category established within scholarship on Flusser, "philosophical fiction" or "scientific fiction," has remained unsatisfactory. It requires updating based on an as-of-yet absent dialog with science fiction studies. Such updating should benefit from the passage of time because Science Fiction (SF) or speculative fiction, as a research field in literary and cultural studies, endured a comparable outlier status, just like *What If?* in Flusser scholarship. More specifi- cally, I suggest that *What If?* belongs to the subcategory of SF Bruce Sterling inaugurated in 1989, that same year *Angenommen* was pub- lished. *What If?* is slipstream fiction. Here's why.

The stories in *What If?* are subsumed under three rather expan- sive themes: family, economics, and politics. Fittingly, the first part, family, encompasses an entire household, including grandparents, a son, brothers, a great-uncle even, and great-grandchildren. The sec- ond part, economics, addresses particular pockets of production in modern economic structures such as the chemical industry, engineer- ing, foreign aid, population growth, and cultivation. The third part embraces the many forms of political activity, from war to peace, from revolution to democracy, from obedience to human rights. To the hurried reader this is mildly intriguing to blatantly tedious. Upon some text mining, together with the Greenhouse Studios team and based on characters, themes, and symbols or visuals,[13] however, the content of *What If?* reveals itself as squarely in the speculative fiction genre, described by Marek Oziewicz as "non-mimetic fiction operating across different media for the purpose of reflecting on their cultural role, especially as opposed to the work performed by mimetic, or real- ist narratives"[14]:

> Characters: meet a futurologist, a terrorist, astronauts, the god-
> dess Venus, hunters, Neanderthals, ghosts or spirits, a very cogent

fetus, Taenia Solium (that tapeworm), the Great Khan Timur the Lame, the Romans, the Goths, an Anhalt-Lippe descendent, "feral" children, Homo Immaterialis, survivalist monks, the Actor-Player-Dealer (possibly all one and the same), the Prophet, Darius (king of all Aryans and Non-Aryans), a Black activist—and all the other protagonists mentioned earlier.

Themes: explore the singularity as the end of humanity; birth/rebirth, excess, *rationes seminales,* technological failure; the meaning of life in the Jewish tradition; compassion versus aggression; spiritualism and determinism; devolution of "culture"; information, datafication, classification; love and self-love, parasitism; Ethno/Eurocentrism, the pitfalls of capitalism; environmentalism, humanity versus its own creations; art versus nature, animism; particle/wave fields, the fog of the past; Darwinism; sensory perception, hearing/seeing; Buddhism; the Quran; democracy viewed as flawed in the future; a new color theory to critique white supremacy.

Symbols/Visuals: imagine charts, graphs, knots, lines, curves, guns, magnets, iron shavings; white clouds, a yellow ocean, an erection, mountains, many instances of the goddess Venus; cramped alleyways, a prayer coat, a library, a dictionary; human-like creatures, burials, hunters; a congress of spirits; paradise inside the womb; destroyed cities, mutilation of human bodies, razor blades; roads as ribbons, cars as stinking boxes, a river of consumer goods; giant cows; hymenoptera; fields, waves, particles, networks; a mushroom cloud, nuclear winter, an unpredictable "curve" with multiple outcomes; telematic screens, buttons (history at our fingertips); hands, feet, nuclear/civil war, overpopulated continents, planetary colonization, centralized computing systems; "Mene mene tekel upharsin"; Ouroboros snake eating its tail; the Peacock throne.

I have my favorites, and so might you. That *Bibliophagus convictus?* A wicked insect of mind-blowing proportions, literally, with a devilish grin to boot. The several "reports" by groups of ethnologists,

scientists or explorers of some ilk? They veer on the Kafkaesque, remi-
niscent indeed of Kafka's 1917 stirring "A Report to an Academy." Some
take several reads, as if resistant to interpretation, oblique, your eyebrows cocked; some are horrific, murderous children, induced
catastrophes for world-cleansing, and organizing humanity in neat
bidecadials. Yet others conjure up vortices that weave a complex mixture of space-time dimensions, catapulting the reader into an
alternate past or distant and alien future. None are related to another.
And yet, they all are spinning within a network of humans, nonhu-
mans, ideas, issues, events, and time that speaks to versions of
realities as much on our minds now as they were when *What If?* was
first published. It still sends a message from back then, more than
thirty years ago, into our pandemic-stricken, divisive, weird and elec-
trifying time.

Why read *What If?*, a text very much of the postmodern, 1989,
moment, in the twenty-first century? Flusser's popular book on
design, *The Shape of Things* (1999), includes a story on "The Submarine."[15] The submersible, an underwater-travel design emerging from
the nineteenth century, becomes the ultimate expression of modernist
warfare in World War I. It, too, in Flusser's slipstream, presents imagination gone awry, because it represents a nineteenth-century dream
that turns into a twentieth-century nightmare. The submarine in this
story functions as a lab for seventeen scientists, artists, and theolo-
gians who leave society for an experiment to rule the world and
anchor on the bottom of the Pacific Ocean ("near the Philippines") to
"enforce the military and intellectual disarmament of humanity."[16] To
be brief, this form of totalitarianism does not succeed. The scientists
fail because they set out to realize utopian ideals based on logic and
control—from the narrator's perspective several hundred years prior
to writing this story—not because the materials did not obey or hold
up, but because the people didn't. Everyone turns against them. The
narrator argues that the experimenters failed because they refused,
deluded, to see an object for what it was: twentieth-century humans
living in a dream world where the common "walking cane presented
an electromagnetic field or a cultural product or a fabrication or a
sexual symbol or a thing proving being *(Dasein)*, in short, within which

it presented everything: except a cane." At the end of such a dream, or nightmare, and upon awakening, lies reality. But, as the narrator acknowledges, the experimenters valiantly sought to "merge faith, knowledge, and art" for the first time since the Middle Ages, while, in their "ephemeral world domination from within the submarine," they inadvertently failed to take into account the human factor. This is a factor that eludes design.

With *What If?*, and, by extension, other texts such as "The Submarine" as well as *Vampyroteuthis Infernalis,* Vilém Flusser aligns himself with some of the best features of slipstream SF, this subcategory of speculative fiction. While the genre itself stays in dispute, Sterling's term has stuck; in fact, according to Victoria de Zwaan, science fiction studies "demonstrates a strangely persistent attachment to the term 'slipstream' that remains hard to explain."[17] Even if Sterling identified it as no more than a certain "sensibility," de Zwaan's list of characteristics and adjacent terminology speaks to slipstream's relevance for placing *What If?* within this genre's contexts: estrangement; late capitalism; postmodernist (experimental) fiction; disruptive; contemporary realities; quasi-SF; uncanny; weird; counterrealism. Flusser should be in good and quite familiar company. While contemporary authors considered slipstream include Kathy Acker, Thomas Pynchon, or Ishmael Reed—authors Flusser never read—among the literary giants influencing slipstream, based on a rare slipstream-scholarship consensus, are Franz Kafka and Luis Borges. Flusser very much read the first, and his imaginary worlds have been repeatedly compared to the second.

What If?: The Future

May the futurologist and the terrorist meet only in Flusser's field of possibilities.

WHAT IF . . .

. . . a terrorist is running across the landscape with a machine gun. He is running toward the future. A futurologist calculates the terrorist's trajectory on his computer and finds that it is headed toward the present. Eventually these two paths cross. The terrorist jumps out from the landscape (out of the computer) onto the futurologist's desk and says, "Unfortunately, I have to shoot you because you stand in the way of the future." Then he pulls the trigger. The futurologist, if he could still speak, might say, "I reckoned that this might happen."

We may call the knot just described the "dialectics of freedom."

This knot can be untangled. There are two knotted perspectives of the future. The terrorist anticipates the penetrability of the future because he *perceives* it and runs into it, whereas the futurologist is *detached* because he sits and waits for it to arrive. The futurologist is the more powerful of the two. Because he can be contemptuous of the terrorist, given the improbability that he will get shot, he can also describe precisely the terrorist's contemptibility. The futurologist can do this because he *presupposes* the future. The terrorist is *merely engaged* in it.

The presupposed future is a field of possibilities that surrounds the present. It pulls individual possibilities from the present to become reality. At first glance, it looks like a magnetic field with iron filings. Still, a field theory of the future is impossible. Not because the theoretician can be stabbed to death by an iron filing like the futurologist by the terrorist, as magnetism works similarly, but because future possibilities bend away (become impossible), become bundled, and in the process strengthen or are nullified. They may even run in a direction opposite to the present. Iron filings are incapable of performing such ontological somersaults. The field of possibilities behaves more like a congress of ghosts: some materialize, others make pacts with or conspire against each other, while still others disintegrate.

By supposing that a particular possibility becomes more probable the closer it moves toward the present, the futurologist is able to manipulate the ghosts. Because proximity is measurable, a computer may project the possibilities more precisely as converging, diverging, or crossing curves. The scenario is improved whenever more data are available. The scenario's degree of probability thus increases, and the margin of error decreases and becomes increasingly measurable. Because we can intervene in this scenario, we can manipulate the supposed future, that is, freedom of choice.

All well and good, but creepy—as is usually the case with ghost stories. The category of *closeness* (proximity) gives us shivers since it means "close to the present," that is, "close to me in the here and now." But I am not all alone in the here and now; others are standing around me, each embedded in their own future. Should I indeed dismiss as improbable everything that concerns others but not me because the future as such is of no concern to me the more distant the possibilities are from my own viewpoint? Because out there they become ever more improbable? We can only accept the category of proximity when we include in it the love of others.

However, a future shared between all others (including myself) has a disadvantage. This grey zone of all individual futures does not possess a horizon. Death has been ruled out. That's why I cannot recognize myself or anyone else in this grey, increasingly calculable future. The series of scenarios introduced here does not exclude death, that is, it does not forgo self-awareness and appreciation of the other. That's why it will refrain from precise calculation.

There are further reasons. At issue in the grey future of the futurologist are calculations of probability. A human being, however, is an animal that is nurtured by the improbable. And that's why the unseasoned soup of the futurologist is unpalatable. The series of scenarios introduced here promises to be flavorful. It will project improbabilities.

Probability is a chimera, its head is true, its tail a suggestion. Futurologists attempt to compel the head to eat the tail *(ouroboros)*. Here, though, we will try to wag the tail.

From the perspective of the futurologist, the future is an adventure *(advenire,* to arrive); that does not hold true for the terrorist—and we should take note of that. The series presented here shares the perspective of the futurologist: it will be adventurous. This promise should make the reader curious. Curiosity motivates all speculation about the future, all presuppositions about the future. The terrorist is not curious, he is engaged. His motives are different, less theoretical.

Curiosity, however, is unreasonable. It tries to jump from today into tomorrow. That is impossible. Wherever you are, that's where you'll find today. This series, motivated by curiosity, represents an unreasonable endeavor, it is an invitation to an impossible journey.

PART I

SCENES FROM FAMILY LIFE

GRANDMOTHER

Once we pierced the whitish cloud cover with its occasional flashes of ball lightning, the planet's surface appeared as a yellowish ocean. It seems stagnant and viscous. One phenomenon fascinates us: the shadow of our airplane is not reflected optically but in bas-relief, and it does not follow the flight path but seems to hasten ahead, as if guiding us. We don't, in fact, follow the precalculated orbit but deviate from it just a bit, as if attracted by a power that our instruments cannot register. The arousal taking hold of us suggests that this power must be Reich's orgone. Toward the horizon indicated by our shadow, a mountain-like formation arises: solid bubbles emerging from the ocean. At the center of the formation, there is a mountain much larger than those that encircle it. There are nine mountains divided into two groups, and the second mountain of the outer group is encircled by a strange ring. Without doubt, the mountainous formation is a model of the planetary system. It begs the following question: "Where do you come from?" We start the engines and head toward the third mountain of the inner group, the one known as Earth. Immediately, the second mountain of this group, Venus, rolls toward the Earth mountain, merges with it, and the mountainous formation is submerged into the ocean again.

Trembling with arousal, we lower a probe onto the ocean's surface to extract a drop to be analyzed. This touch transforms the surface, which had been stagnant and undifferentiated, into a storm-driven tidal wave with white-capped waves. Each wave seemed to want to grab us. We accelerate and just barely escape the marine tremor. Once we disengage the storm subsides. Our analysis of the drop shows the following: 21.5 percent margaric acid and olein; 15 percent vitelline, 8.5 percent phosphoric substances, 0.5 percent cholesterol, 0.3 percent cerebrine, and traces of sodium chlorine, calcium, dyes, and finally 51 percent water. The ocean planet consists of egg yolk.

Hypothesis: Venus is an egg, and the cloud covering we pierced is the egg white. We are currently located in the zona pellucida. The pole that attracts us is the embryonic disk that contains the cell nucleus. And the Venusian tremor we just survived is the transformation of the outer egg layers in preparation for receiving sperm. Soon, the formational yolk and the yolk bed will together move and break away from the planet's pole with the power of millions of volcanoes in order to devour us. But Venus is a thinking egg (just take a look at the model of the solar system it suggested). We should be able to devise a code that might help dissuade her from taking us for a spermatozoon.

We fire our rockets twice, then, after a pause, three times, then five times. A new formation immediately appears on the planet's surface: the well-known triangle with the squares on each side. Pythagoras as a response to arithmetics. The Pythagorean theorem trembles. A theoretical orgasm?

We switch the code and agree on the Jungian version of archetypes. We converse like two lovers, like two mating animals. The course of our conversation cannot be depicted in words, in numbers, or digitally. But its result can be narrated: Venus reveals itself as the aphrodisiacal world aspect, and we are illuminated by her venereal ray of love and beauty. Bountiful enthusiasm elates us, and all theoretical information stored within is thereby heightened and given new meaning.

Geographically and historically, Venus can be located as a hierophany. She is Semitic (Ishtar, Ashtoreth, Astarte, Belit, Mylitta, Al-ilat) or an ocean monster (fish woman), a celestial appearance (sun and/or moon woman), she is bellicose (Areia), peaceful (Apostrophia), and she is the second planet in our solar system. But as a goddess she is omnipresent: the Great Urania in the atomic nucleus, Pandemos in the galaxies, Anadyomene in the origin of life, Euploia in the origin of biological species. In death, she is Tymorychos, and beyond death she is Epitymbia. She is the forming principle Morpho, the Beautiful. She radiates beauty, Pasiphae, but she remains the Dark, Melainis. She is the eternal feminine that attracts us.

Ecstatically orgasmic, we plummet into the opening pole of the planet, into the cell nucleus of the Ur-egg, into the opening womb of Aphrodite Genetrix, the Great Mother. We rush headlong into love-death to fertilize the Great Mother as the logos spermatikos ejaculated from Earth, to incorporate into her genetic information the logical information gained on Earth, to exalt all terrestrial culture (science, technology, art, philosophy, politics) into the eternal organic, into the holy. We plummet into the goal of human history, into the *abundance of time*.

Before we let ourselves fall, we have to convey our glad tidings to there from whence we issued. The NASA computers, however, are unable to decipher such gospels. Thankfully, there is competition to space travel on Earth. Its calculators are called prayer wheels, and they are programmed to process myths. Therefore, our news must be sent to Lhasa. In Lhasa, the image of the goddess is to be unveiled for humanity so that earthly creatures may rise toward love and beauty. Om.

THIRD SCENARIO

GRANDFATHER

Until recently, the Bom-Retiro quarter consisted of an
entanglement of Jewish alleyways. Portuguese and Yiddish shouts
connected the sidewalks. Hawkers wearing *payot* in caftans pitched
blue jeans; half-naked women pitched themselves. Honking Volkswa-
gens tried to find a way through. Back then, I went there on occasion
to play a game with myself. I tried to guess the origins of the people.
Afterward I made sure I was correct. It was easy for me to distinguish
Sephardim from Ashkenazi, but I had problems separating Smyrneans
from people from Constantinople or Frankfurters from Viennese.
The highpoint of this game—and its end—came about as follows:

An old gentleman wearing a prayer coat and sandals but without
a head cover or sidelocks slowly strode along the alleyway. I could not
categorize him. Even the main categories, Ashkenazi-Sephardi did not
fit. I then addressed him in Portuguese. He politely responded in a
language unknown to me. While I am unfamiliar with Semitic languages, it seemed to me that his language was related to Hebrew the
way Latin is to Portuguese. I rejected this absurd theory in favor of one
more reasonable: the old gentleman probably spoke a Yemenite dia-
lect. He had likely just arrived in São Paulo as he appeared lost. He
needed help. I stopped a taxi and the old gent willingly got in. I told
the driver to take us to the library. There, I wanted to consult a
Yemenite dictionary.

The Yemenite dictionary wasn't any help. I then asked the

librarian for a Chaldean dictionary. While she was searching, I tried to mobilize in my memory the saved chunks I had stored regarding Ur (and to simultaneously free myself of the etymologically misleading smack of German): Kaldi was Semitic; several Babylonian kings (Nabopolassar and his descendants) were Chaldean; the priestly caste of Mesopotamia consisted primarily of Chaldeans; for the classic Ancients the Chaldeans were magicians and astrologers; later, the Chaldean language was mistaken for Aramaic, and as such it has been used by a Christian sect unto the present day. The librarian reemerged, beaming, with an English-Chaldean dictionary. I opened it, sat down in front of the old gentleman who was blinking, amused, and asked: "Abi-ram? Ab-hamon? Ab-rucham? Sarah?" Laughing loudly, he responded: "Abi." There was an unmistakable undertone of authority in his laugh.

I understood: "I am father, you are son, no matter which surname you give me, and I ask you not to invert the roles, please." I handed him the dictionary so that he could lead the conversation instead of me. I knew how risky it would be to oppose him—did he not betray his business partner, and did he not even seek to betray God? Did he not prostitute his wife, and on top of that disinherit his sons in favor of just one? And did he not aim to murder this chosen son? He opened the dictionary and—pointing to the English page opposite the Chaldean words—began to interrogate me:

"Did He actually keep His promise?" I thought he meant "His contract," that thing with the sand on the ocean, and I responded, "There are approximately 16 million Jews, that's how the grandchildren of your grandson Jacob are called, but there are way over 4 billion other people."

He was not interested in statistics (or in Jews). "Did He do better later on than back then with Sarah?"—"As far as I know, He tried three more times. With Rachel, with a certain Mary, and with Mohammed, an Arabian man."—"I know about Rachel. Do tell me about Mary."—"He impregnated her using Gabriel; he became a rabbi, who took the sins of all people upon himself."—"Did that eliminate sin?"—"No, because the people did not really believe in the rabbi and merely simu-lated their faith. And the rabbi did not want to take their freedom of choice from them. He never forced them to follow him."—"And hence the renewed attempt with this Mohammed"?—"Yes. In this case Gabriel dictated a book to him instead of getting someone pregnant."

He laughed and slapped his thighs: "As a second, revised edition of this rabbi?"—"Yes. But this did not really diminish the sum of the world's sins either."

"And apart from that, how have the people carried on since I left?"—"They understood the world better and better. That's how it changed, as you have been able to see."—"Did they do that to improve themselves?"—"Is it not indeed interesting to want to recognize the world as an end in itself?"

He became angry: "Shut up! This is why I left Ur."—"Many people tried to better themselves."—"They wanted to correct the mistakes He had made?"—"Rather, they wanted a better life."—"Did they succeed?"—"They live longer now, suffer less pain, experience more, and have many things at their disposal."—"You idiot! That's what you call a better life?"

I was offended. "Yes. A better life is more life."

He doubled over with laughter. "You think life is an end in itself?"—"There are people who ask about the meaning of life. But the answers are so paltry that I'm ashamed of them."—"Have at it, dear little son!"—"Some think you live for others—without knowing what they live for. Some think you live for the grandchildren and they for their own grandchildren. Again, others think that you live for a future life, and that this one is without meaning. I myself think you live to learn as much as possible."—"And what have you learned?"—"For example, that the world is much bigger and older than you assume." I was furious now. "How much bigger and older?"—"These are dimensions that you cannot even imagine."—"But you, of course, are able to imagine them?"—"No, I can't either."

He choked with laughter. "This is the utter nonsense you learned?"—I couldn't help myself: "This isn't nonsense at all. It produces better cheese than the one for which you betrayed Lot."

Screaming, he stood up: "You think I left Ur to make goat cheese? I curse my seed!" I fell to the floor, put my head in his lap and pleaded:

"Teach me, father, about the meaning of life." His wrath turned to laughter: "A curse, after all, is better pedagogy than a blessing." While he placed his hand upon me, I posed this question: "Please, what is it that makes you laugh so hard?"—"You have no sense of humor. And jokes cannot be explained."

FOURTH SCENARIO

GREAT UNCLE

Publisher's preliminary statement: There have been complaints about the authenticity of the document shared here. We are publishing it because only now—at the turn of the fourth millennium CE (New York time)—can we examine and revoke the incidents reported therein.

To the Ministry of Big Game. Lascaux, Dordogne. The head of the expedition into the Valley of the Neanderthals encloses the following report, respectfully signed.

It was our task to examine the economic significance of the apparently humanoid mammals living along the Neander. They are a group of about seventy individuals: 11 males, 32 females; the young make up the rest. They are shaggy, walk almost erect, their live weight is about 75 kilograms (165 lb.), their height approximately 1.65 meters (5 ft. 4 in.) (because they crouch they appear to be smaller). Their faces are animalistic: flat nose, deep-set eyes below bulging eyebrows, receding forehead, no chin. The skull is elongated and broadens toward the back. The hands are human-like, the feet ape-like. The teeth are typical of herbivores. They appear archaic (even the young look geriatric). Just as archaic are the tools they undoubtedly create themselves. (We decided to call these tools *pattern-like* to distinguish them from human cultural objects.) You will find several samples of stone and bone tools enclosed. The animals emit grunting noises, and several members of the expedition thought to have heard the sound "Yeti." The most confusing observation, however, is that they bury their dead in flower beds. There was divided opinion among the members of the expedition about whether these animals could be hunted. As a result, we are forwarding both opinions to the Ministry for a final decision. The minority group's objections prevented us from adding samples of fur, meat, and bone to this report.

Majority group's report: We had the opportunity to examine two skeletons. Each individual bone is clearly distinct from its human equivalent. The same applies to the skeletons of horses. However, since the general structure of the skeletons is identical to ours, we can conclude that Neanderthals are animals that are more closely related to us than to horses.

Of course, our findings are based primarily on aesthetic and existential considerations. The Neanderthals are repulsively ugly and thick-necked; they grunt, feed on grass, gnaw on twigs and bare their teeth. Some of them may have reached out with their arms in our direction, but most of them fled. It is certain that none of the expedition members felt even the slightest sexual arousal at the sight of the females. It is undeniable that tool production and burial in flower beds is rare in the animal world. This presents us, however, with taxonomic issues, not ethical ones—that is, with the question of how to classify these animals zoologically. In no way are they human, because what is specifically human is the ability to manipulate *concepts* such as "stone," and not the ability to transform that which is designated by the concept. Neanderthals do not think because they do not speak. They are animals.

We therefore suggest that the Ministry declare the Neanderthals to be fair game for economic and ecological reasons. Their fur is particularly suitable for the production of coats, especially since it is available in almost fitting form. And the Neanderthals occupy a niche that is partially in competition with us. They must be removed for philanthropic reasons.

Minority group's report: When we approached the group, an older man walked toward us with open hands. Several children were laughing. The Neanderthals fled only when we did not reciprocate. They shivered with fright. We wish to inform the Ministry that we probably committed a fatal error (a sin). It is true that the Neanderthals are different from us. For example, their skulls are ten percent larger than ours. Because they are different, we perceive them as ugly. However, it is unworthy of humans to elevate this alienating difference, this instinctive repulsion, this lack of sexual attraction to the level of epistemological and classificatory principle. It is worthy of humans to acknowledge difference and to recognize in the Neanderthals another form of humanity. To recognize, for example, that burial in flower beds indicates that the Neanderthals have an attitude toward death that appears foreign to us.

What is important to us is the mutual recognition of the other. Only when we can recognize the Neanderthals as another form of humanity may we be respected by them as human beings in return. And only then will we be able to both see and recognize in our mutually ugly faces that which is completely Other. Instead, we have tried to know and treat the Neanderthals as animals. That empowers us to be the stronger group. We may now hunt them, kill them, and use their fur for coats. As for their part, they cannot no longer acknowledge us; they must now deal with us as beasts of prey. The end of this feedback loop should be obvious: we will eradicate the Neanderthals and enrich ourselves with their fur—and we will become impoverished because we will no longer be able to incorporate a Neanderthal dimension into our being. We will lose the possibility to become other than what we are.

We therefore propose that the Ministry halt this process. We ask that a few Neanderthals be invited to Lascaux so that they may learn of our ways of being with the hope of initiating a fruitful conversation so that together we may stride toward a richer, more human-worthy future.

Decision of the Ministry for Big Game's Study Committee: The expedition's majority report into the Valley of the Neanderthals is accepted.

Publisher's appendix: Neanderthal eggs and sperm are currently in our possession. We can therefore reproduce this species and reverse the decision of the Study Committee. The above document is being published for the purpose of expanded discussion.

FIFTH SCENARIO

BROTHERS

It is my honor to speak at the opening of the first anthropo-
logical conference after the April revolution. Just a few weeks ago,
words such as "anthropology" and "humanism" were frowned upon. It
was forbidden to utter the word "death." We were allowed only to visit
Hegel's grave. Wet nurses who uttered the word "human being," scar-
ing children, were brought into court and accused of spreading
superstition. We had to hand over all images of human beings and
anthropoid apes to the vice squad. Today, we are gathered here to
express our longing for materialization, the power that supports us
mysteriously to the core, in short, our humanism. (Roaring applause)

The officially sanctioned spiritism tries to prove that it is both
impossible and unnecessary to believe in the existence of human
beings. It is absurd to think of a creature that is of the spirit and material at the same time. Spiritism postulates two dialectically opposed
worlds: ours and a material one. Our world, made up of spaceless and
timeless thoughts, is tasked with contemplating the things of space-
time, to detach them from space and time. And we ourselves, who are
nothing but pure knots of thought, exist as the only imaginable life
form: life as a conversation regarding recognition and about that
which has been recognized and become known. The myth according
to which we emerged from human corpses appears to be a primitive
attempt to localize us, and reactionary ideologies such as metempsychosis or reincarnation are to be combated as counterrevolutionary

because—according to official Spiritism—they taint the purity and dignity of the Spirit. However, the Ministry for Enlightenment and Salvation, based on Decree 172/4, was compelled to distance itself a little from official spiritism and now permits anthropology. The impulse toward materialization, apparently, is stronger than all revolutionary ideologies. (Agitated heaving and weaving among the spirits present.)

What, after all, does the purity of the Spirit, praised beyond all measure, consist of? Of the fact that all thoughts, if they are correct, can be reduced to zero. Proof that thoughts are correct consists of identifying them as tautologies. Such dissolution toward zero is the kind of salvation promised to us by the Enlightenment. That is what we must fight against! (Thunderous applause.) At issue is not dancing in graveyards while reciting incantations and jumping on individual graves—as we are accused of doing by the spiritists—(loud laughter in the hall), but about providing content for our thinking and for ourselves. This is not a primitive, reactionary endeavor; it is the essence of the Spirit. I am going to try to provide evidence for this accordingly. I remind the censors present in the hall of the aforementioned Decree, and ask that they please not interrupt me.

The world of the Spirit does not consist of translating things from equations that, assuming they are correct, turn out to be tautologies; rather, it consists of adventure that becomes ever deeper and richer. Every one of us emerged from the death of a human being in order to enrich ourselves by the physical experiences and events of the deceased and to elevate them with recognition and beauty. The conversation that we exemplify clarifies that which has been gained, eliminates the slag of error and lies, and moves it toward logical and mathematical purity. Once this catharsis has ended, we dive back into the human body to learn and experience new things. At the center of this adventure is the human being who lives for us and for whom we think—and who lives in us, within whom we live. Let us pray. (Devout silence)

Far be it from me to subscribe to a materialistic humanism. Quite the contrary, we have to identify ourselves completely—as the Spirit we are—before we can think about becoming materialized. We should not fight spiritism as such, we should fight dogmatic spiritism. And I see a new epoch emerging, out of the current, postrevolutionary darkness, an epoch of self-confident humanism. (Roaring applause)

This self-confident humanism will recognize the world as a process of spiritual unfurling. At first, the Spirit was nothing more than a disposition in the program of life. It lay dormant in the structure of hydrogen atoms. Then it began to articulate in the complex structure of polymeric connections. In the process of living life, it became ever more conscious of itself until it erupted, like a butterfly from its cocoon, in the species *human being.* And as it erupted it started to rotate. It emerged from the dead to dive back into newborns. Thanks to this rotational motion, that is, this metempsychosis, the Spirit now truly confronts the world. The human being is the point of rupture at which the Spirit is freed to overcome the world, and then dive back into it to change it. The human being is the Alpha and Omega of the unfolding of the Spirit. Let us pray. (Devout silence)

We who have broken away from the human being and seek to dive back in are always in danger of losing contact with the experience, to dissipate, to become formal. That's why, in our formal thinking, it is difficult for us to believe in the existence of human beings. The same is true of human beings: they are always in danger of losing contact with us, the Spirit, and to get entangled in concrete things, to become material. That's why it is difficult for human beings, in practice, to believe in our existence. But within us surges an aspirational power that we experience as a longing for thingness, for materialization, for becoming human, and no ideology of any kind can destroy this belief. (Roaring applause) Something comparable is happening within the human being, which also longs to become Spirit, to become us. These two tendencies must, over time, merge. The cycle of the Spirit, from death to rebirth, will become increasingly conscious of itself. The realm of the Spirit and human beings will merge. An immaterial culture will develop.

That is the Utopia I wish to preach to you: the human being as the pivot point for all spirits, each spirit as a pivot point for all human beings. That is my anthropology, my humanism. All of us, ladies and gentlemen, will rotate around each human being. That's why I counter the battle cry of the revolution "Spirits of all kinds unite!" with another one: "Spirits, scatter among human beings!" (The vice squad breaks into the hall and reduces all of those present to zero in order to correct them.)

SIXTH SCENARIO

SON

Please don't despise me because I am so young and small and am making a pitiable impression overall. You may interpret my arched head and neck as a bow, but because I am barely 35 millimeters (1.37 in.) tall, it probably won't be noticed. You are more likely to conclude that I'm just crotchety. Indeed, I don't look toward the future forthrightly because I am hemmed in by casings, skins, and cords; because I roll into myself; and because I have an annoying habit of tickling my nose with my little pecker. By the way, you are not the only one who despises me. My mother decided to abort me. You think this is absurd, a murder, a sin? I'm not willing to go that far. I can't reconcile it with my small (in absolute terms) but, relatively speaking, large brain to toss abortion, coitus with a condom, the drowning of newborns, execution of hardened criminals, the gassing of millions of innocents, and the crucifixion of Jesus into the same bag labeled "Murder." I will therefore try to consider the pros and cons of my dear mother's decision.

She considers me an accident of the kind that can happen during sexual intercourse. The spermatozoon that entered one of my dear mother's eggs may have originated from illegitimate testicles. Since abortion is legal, my dear mother may wish to legalize me by that means. However, I am uncomfortable considering myself an accident (coincidence). The gentleman's sperm's paths are dark and twisted. And yet it is necessary for a spermatozoon to encounter an egg *by accident*? Don't laugh; this is, after all, what the materialist Democritus had in mind with the coincidental and necessary swerving of atoms, for which he used the term "clinamen"—which Lucretius rendered into Latin as "accidens." My mother does believe in a legitimate order that may be disturbed by accidents, but in which it is possible to remove disruptions from the world. I, however, believe that all order is based on accidents like myself. And I am convinced that I see more deeply than my dear mother because I am closer to the origin than she and—more significantly—because my dear unknown father over-sired and over-conceived me. Nonetheless, I don't want to insist on this statement. After all, my dear mother's heart is beating within me.

Do you think my precocity is a bit absurd because it shows that I have no idea of how probability is calculated? Four billion years ago, a molecular structure evolved on some Precambrian beach that held within it, preprogrammed, the accidental encounter of my paternal sperm with my maternal egg. Not only that, if I were not to be aborted, the probability that I would grow up to be a mathematical genius, a mass murderer, or mongoloid idiot would be calculable as well. Right? Accept my fetal arch as a bow to the correctness of your arguments. You are water on my mill. Statistically it is immaterial whether I am aborted or not: the flow of genetic material would not be substantially altered. My dear mother is better at math than yours.

Does this offend you? In great pain, would your own mother have given you extra-uterine life, the beauty of which I cannot fathom? Allow me to disagree with you. The uterus in which I float is warm and cozy; I receive oxygen and nutrition for free. Where I am looks like paradise to those on the outside. I refer you to countless utopias and myths. What have you gained from the traumatic experience of having been born? You were thrown from a physiological into a sociocultural uterus, and not into any kind of freedom. Your birth diploma was nothing more than a preparatory exam for the larger diploma, that is, the doctorate of death. My dear mother collapses the two in me and bestows upon me the doctorate prematurely—honoris causa, of course. The more I argue with you, the more I am convinced that my dear mother will abort me out of love to spare me from suffering.

You claim that life is about gathering experience and then making decisions accordingly. That, supposedly, is freedom. Are you familiar with the theory that at birth 90 percent of one's experiences are already in the past? How often have you decided anything for yourself? Isn't it more accurate to say that you thought a couple of times that you had to make a decision (a curious contradiction, right?), but determined in retrospect that your decision, at that decisive moment, was contingent on circumstance? My dear mother is aborting me so as not to rush me out of paradise into this uncomfortable freedom. The uterus is not as soundproof as generally assumed. I heard some of your songs of praise about freedom. Now that I am about to get my diploma, I recognize in these songs all kinds of dissonances. I prefer a well-tempered clavier.

Please excuse the interruption of our stimulating conversation; I was otherwise occupied. My dear mother suddenly decided to carry me to term; however, she has not changed her opinion of my unimportance, my legitimacy, my future suffering, and the problem of freedom in general. My mother is a good citizen; she never changes her opinion. But the doctor explained to her that an abortion would be detrimental to her own health. And that forces me to reconsider my situation.

I now understand how we—you and I—were mistaken. When we are born the issue is less about accident, coincidence, and necessity, about suffering and paradise, that is, not first and foremost about freedom. The real issue is love. While my mother is ready to carry me to term now out of self-love, is this self-love not also basically a love for me who is a part of her—despite her cynical laughter? Isn't it true that I love her for that, even though I preferred to be aborted? Love is a tricky thing. One should not necessarily trust those who praise maternal love and preach love for their neighbor. But now that I must (and may) be born, I realize that the question of freedom makes sense only when it is positioned within the context of love.

I don't know how we endure the confusion of love with freedom, that is, extra-uterine life. I am still unborn. Maybe being born has only this single purpose: to learn to love and to be tested on it. I see you're laughing again. You are quite right, I've not been spared from abortion; I will be aborted at a later date, just like you. So, being born is useless. At the same time, I now have a bit more time to prepare for my diploma. Please allow me to end our friendly conversation at this point so I may dedicate myself to my dissertation on love and freedom—in order to live.

GRANDCHILDREN

Report to the Environmental Commission at the United Nations: in February, the children of the favelas in Bogotá occupied the inner city under the leadership of a Maoist professor. Subsequent bombing by the air force did not drive them out. (Apparently, the rebels tore their leader to pieces and ate him.) In April, Malinche, a heretofore unknown movement, mobilized Mexico's children to storm the capital. To date, the death count is four million. In May, similar events occurred in São Paulo, Rio, Recife, and Belo Horizonte. The children control the entire area between Santos and Campinas. Recife has been leveled. Youth led by mullahs took over the lower course and the delta of the Nile and captured Cairo. The mutilation of all adults (castration and hand amputations) continues unabated. Similar rebellions are happening in Calcutta, Lagos, and Djakarta. Rebels everywhere consist of five- to fourteen-year-old children of both sexes who grew up on and in garbage heaps, and who are armed with razor blades and fish knives. (Girls occasionally carry babies in their arms.) Physically, they are underdeveloped. Their IQ is close to the level of idiocy. They also carry numerous viruses, some of which have yet to be identified. They display derisive contempt toward all adults. We here limit ourselves to phenomenological observations:

Despite being undernourished and diseased, the children are agile. Effortlessly, they climb up the fronts of skyscrapers. And despite their low IQ, they are nimble. They destroy complex systems such as

cars with one crushing grip. They live in small gangs. They are sexually precocious and have an active sex life that entirely lacks emotion.
They mutilate and murder each other, fight amongst themselves for
drugs, and they unify only when seeking to entrap adults. Their out-
standing mental abilities are brutality, cunning, distrust, and
inventiveness. Their most striking feature is the absence of any stir-
rings of compassion. Shortly after birth they were ejected from the
web of society and grew up parasitically as human waste on inhuman
detritus. For them, all cultural information, like any waste product,
has become blurred and amorphous. This explains their uniformity
throughout the world. They are positioned, like any waste product, at
the transition from culture to nature. They live approximately at the
same level as the Lower Paleolithic, except that they didn't, in fact,
achieve that level from nature, but from industrial culture. Their habi-
tat, metropolitan garbage, requires hunting methods different from
those in the older Stone Age. They do not represent a prehistoric phenomenon, but one that is posthistoric. To recognize them, we
therefore need to create new categories that are different from those
that are outdated. Only when such new categories have become available will we be able to address the problem described here.

We have indeed tried to develop such categories. We concluded
that we have to start with the second law of thermodynamics. From
our perspective, waste, that is, the lifeworld of the children, is an environment that is not only hostile to life, but life-endangering. For those
of us who inhabit culture, life is a negatively entropic process that
stores and processes information, while waste is the opposite of life,
an entropic process that deletes information. The children, however,
have a concept of life that is contrary to ours. To them it is a process
during which information is consumed, that is, eaten and destroyed.
At issue here are two dialectically contradictory concepts of life and
value systems. We inhabitants of culture put a positive value on producing, building, and creativity, while destruction, annihilation, and
dissolution are negative. The children, as inhabitants of waste, think
that quite the opposite is true. For us, culture is *valuable* because it
stores information, and waste is a *non-value* because information is
ground up into something amorphous. For the children, culture is

value-free (as nature is to us) because it is only the start of consumption, and waste is valuable because information is *en-valued*, which means it is utilized and worn out. In short, we are in a fight against the second law of thermodynamics, and the children are in harmony with it.

This formulation allows us to appreciate this new life-form of which the children are emblematic. For example, we begin to understand their derisive contempt toward us and culture, and, likewise, the imaginative passion with which the children destroy cultural objects (such as using rubber tires as fuel and broken windows as weapons). This formulation also allows us to see a solution to the problem the children pose. Culture is to the children what nature is to us, that is, the natural resource of raw material that supports waste. Therefore, the children cannot annihilate us without risking perishing themselves for lack of waste. Should they wish to survive (which cannot be assumed given their engagement with entropy), they will have to tolerate us. Their reflections are not dissimilar from those of our economists: just as they must protect nature, the children will have to protect culture from overutilization.

As a result, we should embrace the following symbiosis between the children and ourselves: thanks to our production of culture, we will provide the waste products vital to them, and they will tolerate this. In formulating this suggested resolution, we realize that such a symbiosis has always characterized the succession of generations. Since the dawn of time, older generations have produced culture in order to be tolerated by the youth. Accordingly, we can report to the Committee that nothing new has occurred since February.

EIGHTH SCENARIO

GREAT-GRANDCHILDREN

We recognize the biological condition of *Homo sapiens*—a species whose males are able to procreate from sexual maturity well into old age, while the female is able to produce eggs periodically only for a short time during her lifespan—reflected in the social structure of the preplanning society. The preplanning society faced two impossible problems: the relationship between male and female, and the even more disastrous problem of trickling, irregular births. The preplanning society perished because of these problems. But even the present planning society is not without its issues. It is the intention of my presentation to make the Ministry of Education aware of one of them, namely, the problem of *creativity*.

At the moment, following the introduction of planned fertilization, society is programmed to expect a life span of eighty years, because this span can be divided into four parts, each of which entails a specific function with regard to creativity. On the first of January of each twentieth year, four hundred million children are born, emerging from sperm and eggs that contained specialized precalculated genetic information. On the same day, fifty million twenty-year-olds are allocated to care for and raise the newborns, while the remaining three hundred and fifty million twenty-year-olds are received by fifty million of the forty-year-olds to be educated. At the same time, the remaining three hundred and fifty million of the forty-year-olds are received by fifty million sixty-year-olds to continue the ongoing creative dialog and to complete projects, while the remaining three hundred and fifty million sixty-year-olds retire, that is, start to enjoy the information that has been developed. At that same moment, four hundred million eighty-year-olds enter euthanasia facilities to die with dignity. The diversion of 12 percent of one generation toward the next presents political problems that have not yet been completely resolved. But this is not my topic. What is of interest here is the distribution of a society into four not quite intersecting cultures.

The planning society presumes that humans live as a society to produce new information, to store it, to hand it on, and to consume it. (When we still had mothers and fathers; that is, lived under the constraints of the preplanning society's chaotic structures, no one really knew which level of culture they occupied). That's why we programmed life to consist of four times twenty years: the first twenty serve to receive cultural information; the second to store it; the third serve to develop new information; and the fourth to take pleasure in the fruits thereof. Creativity is limited to the ages between forty and sixty. However, increasingly it appears that it may not be a good idea to reduce creativity biographically to such a degree. This realization rocks the entire structure of the planning society. There is some risk of returning to the chaotic situation of the preplanning society. To confront this risk, it is necessary to contemplate the creative process.

Theoretically speaking, we must distinguish between two types of creativity, the variational and the transcendental. Variational creativity connects already-existing information such that new information is created. Transcendental creativity integrates foreign elements (noise) into already-existing information to result in new information. While the preplanning society veiled both types of creativity, especially the transcendental, in myths like inspiration, intuition, and genius, the planning society has been able to program and manage creativity ever since the formulation of theories of gaming and decision-making, and since the invention of artificial intelligence. The drawback here is that it is impossible to clearly distinguish the two types of creativity from each other, or for that matter variational creativity from information storage. It is this fuzziness of the creative process that threatens to overthrow society's entire scaffolding.

The forty- to sixty-year-olds guide the twenty- to forty-year-olds in their culture on how to store previously developed information in memory. By necessity, this information is stored variably. Errors emerge that lead to the inclusion of noise. That's why this culture is creative, even if that is not the intent of the societal program. In their culture, the forty- to sixty-year-olds develop new information, and noise from previous information is included intentionally. The result is usually failure, largely redundancies: additional chess pieces complicate the rules without making the game more interesting. This culture, then, turns out to be less creative than that of the younger generation. The sixty- to eighty-year-olds absorb with pleasure the information developed, which, surprisingly, creates new information—partly because of consumption, partly because of redistribution. The actual situation is as follows: the younger and older generations are more creative than planned; they are even more creative than the generation that is supposed to be exclusively creative, according to the plan. The grey zones between generations blur societal structures. Generational conflicts are increasingly an issue, and we anticipate an uprising by the twenty-year-olds.

The biological contingency of *Homo sapiens* guaranteed an (empirical) connection between the generations in the preplanning society, as back then, fathers and mothers were needed to beget children. By the way, this necessity was reflected in the human psyche, as is evident in old documents, like Freudian ones. Ever since human beings became de-biologicized, this generational connection can no longer be taken for granted. The social consensus currently consists in the conviction that creativity is society's only purpose. Were this consensus to fall apart because of the murkiness of the concept *creativity*, we would anticipate a return to the animalistic and bestial; in short, we would revert to a biological state. The Ministry of Education will have to plan revolutionary projects for the future.

PART II

SCENES FROM ECONOMIC LIFE

ECONOMIC MIRACLE

Because I cannot express myself independently, my host will do it for me.[1] As such, it will contribute to the critique of Expressionism. Let's leave it at that. Allow me to introduce myself. My name is *Taenia solium*,[2] but I am neither exclusively female nor of Roman origin. My appearance is elegant and elongated. My head (scolex) is shaped like a ball and comes equipped with suction cups and hooks; my body, which measures 3.5 m (11 ft. 5 in.), consists of 1,500 phalluses (male readers will justifiably turn pale with jealousy). Each phallus (proglottid) contains complex ambisexual apparatuses: approximately 50,000 eggs and the accompanying sperm. Accordingly, I accommodate around 75 million individuals within me. Indeed, I consider myself a single being and a society all at once. As an individual, I live in the constant joy of love. As a society, I follow love's commands.

Economically speaking, I am completely satisfied. I am delivered from all such worries, because my body's skin (cuticle) only absorbs nutrients already digested by my hosts. I am fully aware that the economic arrangement is complex (my host must labor to acquire my food from the environment, chew it, and digest it), but trustingly and without a care, I adapt to this regime. I know, too, that I trouble my hosts on occasion, but this is none of my concern. I am dedicated to love. As you may have noticed, I am fully pubescent. However, I shouldn't try to hide my somewhat confused past life. I was born when my parent's lowest phallus came loose from its body and was excreted with its host's feces *(non olet)*.[3] Back then, I was as small as an egg and developed independently into a larva with a hook. I am proud to have been an autodidact. By happenstance, a pig came by (chance and destiny mesh) and ate me together with the feces. I then migrated through the body of my alternate host into its eyeball. I was well taken care of there even though I must have caused discomfort. I am grateful to my host. I grew to become a fluid-filled tapeworm larva with an invaginated head, and, after this introspective phase, I migrated into the musculature of my alternate host. My current host purchased me as pork in a supermarket. I migrated into his intestines and assumed my present form of existence, filled entirely with love. Freed of economic concerns, I became pure love.

For two reasons, I may consider myself a model for a future human society. The first is Darwinian. The well-understood goal of a life cycle is to produce a human being whose task it is to host me. Consequently, I am the actual purpose of the life cycle. The human being must emulate me. The second reason demands closer examination, as it demands of human beings an *imitatio taeniae*.

Human beings have recognized the economy as the substructure of sex only since they separated and redeemed sex from the economy (libido from procreation). The only justification of economic life (of platonic *ascholía*) consists in serving as a foundation for sex (platonic *eros*). It is even apparent to human beings that all busyness (business) aims toward creating leisure *(scholé)*—a leisure that makes it possible to devote oneself to pure, unencumbered love (just as it is stipulated in the sanctification of the Sabbath in Judeo-Christianity). In order to subordinate the economy to love it is necessary to identify everything economic as being of inferior value, that is, too unworthy of one's existential interest. That's how humanity began: labor is automated. The work ethic begins to yield to a new sexual ethic—a beginning still hesitant and inadequate.

Unfortunately, sex is distributed among human beings across two separate organisms. That's why they are forced to develop technologies that allow for an encounter between these two organisms. Human sex life is bound by technologies, which means work. For humans, *pure love* is possible only in the form of masturbation. The disadvantage of masturbation is that self-love represents a closed circle and, consistent with the second law of thermodynamics, tends to become entropic. That's how we must understand the Ancients' attempts to bring about pure love by means of homosexuality— experiments that are justifiably rejected by those motivated by economics. Such approaches are doomed to fail because they differ from the heterosexual by their economic uselessness alone, not because they are freed from technology. Only when human beings have attained my own sexual complexity will they be able to liberate themselves economically and live in pure love.

Each of my phalluses can copulate with itself, each of my phalluses can copulate with another one, and each of my phalluses can copulate with another *Taenia*. The variability in types of orgasms is so vast that even the most advanced computer is incapable of calculating their capacity. The peristaltic movements of my host, this completely automated economy from my point of view, beat the rhythm to the creative symphony of love I compose incessantly. Thanks to this orgiastic, ever-interweaving fugal composition, I am following a self-evident command to love others like myself and to love myself like all others. This is how I honor the supreme command: "Amor muove il sole e le altre stelle."[4] Cosmic peristalsis.

It is incumbent upon you humans to emulate me by overcoming the economy, thereby moving closer toward the goal of life that I exemplify: parasitism.

FOREIGN AID

The desperate calls for foreign aid from the inhabitants of the distant Western Peninsula who have been sitting in jail cells, shaken by torture, compelled us to send an expedition of three shamans into the crisis area. Yesterday, they returned to Oymyakon. This is their report:

This distant Western Peninsula, a peripheral region protruding into the Atlantic, is carved up into subpeninsulas and islands, crisscrossed by mountainous areas and valleys, and traversed by rivers in all directions. A bay, the Mediterranean, extends far into the landmass. For these reasons, serious nomadic animal husbandry has been impossible. The inhabitants were forced to plant grasses and get settled. Because of repeated waves of immigration from the heartland, each new wave was layered upon the previous, as in geological formations. As a result, the original ethnic stratification gave way to a more social one. The ethnic and social tensions that arose time and time again caused chaotic upheavals, that is, *national wars* and *social revolutions*. Repeated attempts were made to impose order and facilitate a halfway decent life. The most successful was the vitalism of the Roman Empire, an organization based on the ideology of plant cultivation, not unlike a khanate. The attempt failed, ultimately, because it was assumed that they had to protect themselves from us. In fact, several expeditions back then—for example, one led by someone the Goths called Attila—tried to eradicate the epidemic at its far-western focus, but in vain. They had to abandon the Peninsula to its miserable fate.

Without a doubt, the real reason for the prevailing misery is the spirit that has gripped the inhabitants of the Peninsula. Originating in Palestine (a small Mediterranean country), this spirit possessed them and called itself Jesus. Apparently, it was a hybrid of Jehovah and a spirit called Logos. Our shamans were not quite successful in identifying the two of them, but the spirit Jesus led in the possessed to seizure-like contortions, less of the body than in their thinking. In fact, Jesus created a confusion of the senses. On the one hand, the possessed believed the senses to be capable of perceiving reality (empiricism) and, on the other hand, that reality is structured in accordance with the rules of thought (rationalism). From this paranoid insanity, the possessed generated a method called "science," and out of it there emerged a black magic they called "technology." The results of this magic are incredible, and they were witnessed and documented by the expedition. Here are some examples:

The distant Western Peninsula is littered with cultish magical artifacts such that it is well-nigh impossible for people to bridge them and encounter each other. For example, broad bands run across the landscape; on festive occasions, they form endless slow-moving lines consisting of innumerable smelly, rattling magic boxes. Victims awaiting development sit in these boxes. In another example, our shamans realized what had led to this complication:

As mentioned, the inhabitants of the Peninsula live off of grasses, but also off of the ruminants that feed on these grasses. It is therefore no wonder that their black magic concentrated on grasses and ruminants. The outcome is a never-ending cornucopia of flour, fruit, wine, butter, and meat, flooding the entire area. The population is in danger of drowning in this torrent, although there are attempts to contain it in huge buildings. Murmured ritualistic formulas, such as "price control" or "common market," attempt to halt this stream, but because these formulas, too, have been infused by the spirit, they produce continuous excess. Our shamans recognized the intent of the Western spirit, namely, to drown its victims in excess.

Another, equally impressive kind of possession is exemplified by a strange, magic button that has been mounted in many places. When it is pressed, a section of the area is flooded by a peculiar light called "electric." This light is entirely superfluous, of course, as we are not the only ones who don't miss it; even the Peninsula inhabitants demanded it only after it had been *invented,* in other words, after it had been infused by the Occidental spirit. Now the people have become totally dependent on this superfluous light. Minutes-long interruptions of this flood of light renders them desperate. The spirit has successfully made those it possesses so dependent on excess that they currently find themselves in the following dilemma: if brakes are applied to this excess, they will perish; if it keeps pace, they will drown in it.

This description does not begin to describe the desperately complicated situation of the Peninsula, because it is becoming increasingly clear that the spirit that dwells therein threatens to break out in distant territories and enthrall new victims. The distant Western Peninsula is the center of an epidemic that has already infected large parts of the earth. Many are in danger of falling prey to this insanity, because the spirit of Jesus takes on ever more fantastic shapes, such as that of *disciplined doubt,* of *progress,* and of *political freedom.* It is therefore increasingly difficult to understand.

Our shamans nonetheless insist that they can exorcize it. However, such remediation efforts would require violent measures. The patient might even die in the process. We thus recommend that the Council of Tribes consult the spirit of our Great Khan, Timur the Lame, in this matter. We believe without a doubt that it is becoming more urgent with every passing day to free humanity from this demon that has gripped the far Western Peninsula, currently best known as "Western culture."

MECHANICAL ENGINEERING

NEW DELHI: The railroad system around Calcutta was catastrophically congested yesterday. The Railroad Ministry, however, is withholding all information.

MADRAS: In the presence of journalists, Swami Vivekamurti called for a protest march against the desacralization of cows in Calcutta.

NEW DELHI: The prime minister summoned the ambassadors of the United States of America and of the Union of Socialist Soviet Republics to his office for secret negotiations.

CALCUTTA: The government seeks to emphasize that "Superkali" is not a cow, but a significant achievement of Indian genetic research.

BOMBAY: Professor Tschandra Mahakananda of the Institute of Genetics declared that Superkali is an artificial mutation of the zebu. It weighs 2,000 tons and consists primarily of a digestive apparatus with integrated artificial intelligence. Superkali, Mahakananda continued, consumes 800 tons of hay and 31,700 gallons of water daily, but produces 18,500 gallons of certified raw milk and 500 tons of manure. Moreover, it is an excellent supplier of urine and gas. In answer to questions by international media it was confirmed that Superkali is currently housed in a hangar connected to the rail system. For further questions Mahakananda referred the attending journalists to his "cowboys" (assistants), who refused to offer any information on the matter, however.

TEL AVIV: A spokesperson for the Weizmann Institute confirmed that hay will soon be synthesized from ocean water.

BUFFALO: At the inauguration of the American Universal System Centrally Applied Cow (AUSCAC), the president declared that "the project's udders produce 237,750 gallons of milkshakes daily. Furthermore, the cloaca supplies 6,000 tons of heating and construction material. The AUSCAC gases will provide energy for the entire state of New York." The president conferred the Distinguished Service Award on the project's two initiators, Professors Sakuro Watanabe (Harvard) and Chaim Mandelstam (Yale). Both scientists had again provided proof for America's pioneer spirit.

GENEVA: The police forcibly dispersed a large demonstration organized by "Antigreen Peace" against the transformation of substantial areas in Europe into grassland.

ROME: It has just been announced that the Vatican is working on an encyclical entitled "De animalibus." Reliable sources have confirmed that the new encyclical contains the following sentence: "We observe with grave concern the sinful attempts to interfere with the divine order of fauna."

NEW YORK: At today's general session of the United Nations, Argentina demanded a change in the composition of the Security Council. The Security Council is to take account of the new power configuration. Only delegates from grass-rich countries are to be seated on the Security Council. There was tumult in the plenary session as the Saudi Arabian delegation physically attacked the Argentinean delegation.

KRASNY: At the inauguration of the Lenin's Meadow super combine, the first secretary of the Central Committee, Comrade Krawkow, noted that the output of the Soviet project will surpass that of the American project by 7.8 percent. The advantages of the Soviet system have now been definitively proven. The Cossack celebration that followed the first secretary's speech took place without horses.

BONN: The "angel cow" installed in Magdeburg (GDR/East) has been outfitted with a suction apparatus designed to absorb grass from the Federal Republic of Germany (FRG/West). The Federal Republic's permanent representative to the German Democratic Republic (GDR) has, in the name of the Federal Republic, issued a formal protest with the agencies in charge in East Berlin.

ATHENS: As agreed by the organizing committee, this year's Olympic Games will be held under the motto "Aphrodite, the cow-eyed." As reported by usually well-informed sources, this is not a reference to super cows but rather emphasizes the cultural heritage of Athens.

PARIS: The Swiss Alp Dream project has received the International Design Prize, awarded for the first time by the École Supérieure des Beaux-Arts. The project will be installed on the Place de la Concorde, replacing the obelisk. Food will be fed into Alp Dream via the Champs Élysées, and according to the jury this will create an organic connection with the Étoile. The mayor of Paris has already endorsed this project. Alp Dream exhibits the hyperrealistic structure of a super cow. The artwork enchants primarily by its ironic references to the alpine economy.

XIANGFAN: "The extent of the accident has been immensely exaggerated," according to a spokesperson from Hupeh province who addressed the press. The media coverage by the "capitalist gutter press" has played a despicable role in this matter. Although there was never cause for concern, words such as "super cow" had spread considerable fear around the world. The flood of manure is now under control. It cost 723 human lives. Members of an expert commission who just returned from the site of the disaster report that we can count on an above-average harvest because of unexpectedly thorough fertilization.

LONDON: Sheapskin, the Labour delegate, pleaded for an additional super sheep project in the House of Commons. Sheapskin described in colorful terms the advantages of a new super sheep. In particular, he emphasized its environmental friendliness. The super sheep would also be more English than the continental projects. Approbation expressed by government officials present invited shrill protest from the opposition ("Shame!"). In the end, both parties agreed to put out a white paper.

OSAKA: The gas explosion that took place last night in the cow installation near Kobe has not yet been contained. The public has been equipped with gas masks. There are no victims to mourn.

MEXICO CITY: News from the remote province of Oaxaca is sparse. Fact is that the super cow's teeth crushed the workers who were temporarily closing the installation following the temporary interruption in the hay supply. As far as we know, the tongue, approximately twelve kilometers long, is circling the area relentlessly. Photos taken by helicopter show images of indescribable destruction.

LOS ANGELES: Concerning the latest reports from Mexico, the director of the Neurophysiology Institute at the University of California, Professor R. Schleiermacher, commented, "Nothing but an old wives' tale." Under no circumstances can this be considered the cow's intention. By and large, these are controllable reflexes. At the same time, Schleiermacher warned not to anthropomorphize the behavior of the super cow.

MUNICH: Patent examiners at the European Patent Office are currently debating the legal distinction between a super cow and a turbo cow. In the United States, the sixth generation of super cows birthed a turbo cow, which was awarded a patent by the authorized office in Washington. No objections were raised. Munich, however, is more hesitant. Although all species of super cows that have required a patent have so far received one, the turbo cow represents an entirely novel "cow invention." Patent protection probably cannot be awarded for such a "novel cow." Ethical or moral considerations played no role in the Munich patent examiners' decision. Whether the application for patent protection is granted will be decided within the next few weeks.

HYDERABAD: Yesterday, the supposedly decommissioned super cow of Aurangabad started to lick up and devour people from the surrounding villages. Villagers escaped in all available vehicles, apart from ox carts. All of the country's temples are overflowing with worshippers. The cows are receiving flower offerings. In the meantime, people are appealing for a neutron bomb.

WASHINGTON: Yesterday's decision by the European Patent Office in Munich has generated protest in the U.S. It is quite probable that the inventor of the turbo cow and the European licensee will appeal the decision. If it is rejected in the end, secret plans appear to exist in the drawers of the laboratories involved.

NEW YORK: Reports of catastrophes from all over the world are flooding news rooms. The simultaneous collapse and eruption of numerous super cows has resulted in millions of casualties in Africa, China, the Soviet Union, and Europe. Now the United States is affected as well. As was just announced, an explosion in Hoboken cut off power lines to Manhattan. New York has been ordered to evacuate at 3 o'clock this afternoon.

AGRICULTURE

The commission instituted by the princely government of Anhalt-Lippe[1] to research the current state of agriculture has submitted its report. The head of the commission, Comrade Prof. Dr. rer. Nat. Dr. h.c. Danton Friedemann, summarized the topic of "artificial fertilizer" as follows:

Whether we fertilize naturally or artificially depends on our definition of *nature* and *art*.[2] We started with the most obvious one. Art is every phenomenon that bears traces of human information. By elimination, all remaining phenomena are to be viewed as nature. Unfortunately, we came to the conclusion that there can be no nature under such a definition. Not only would all human beings be artificial creatures because all hold inherited as well as acquired information and are thus *cultural factors*—except our noble Prince Eberhard XC, whom no one can accuse of cultural infection. In addition, all presumably natural factors would prove to be artificial ones. Even the moon shows traces of the cosmonauts' soles. If the governing party of the Fundamentalist Greens wanted to act in accordance with its program and allow only nature to exist—they would have to remove the moon, which is as of now beyond the capabilities of the principality. And so we saw ourselves obliged to look for another definition of nature and art.

For this purpose, we consulted a foreigner's body of thought, the Breisgau native Martin Heidegger. This approach showed that "everything that has its origin in itself is natural. Everything else is to be called *artificial*." Yet, even this excursion into the (admittedly diseased) Black Forest proved to be unproductive. In our critical analysis of the man from Breisgau we were forced to admit that "being" *(sein)* is a verb, with a future tense of "that which is present to us" *(das uns Anwesende)*, with a present tense of "our being here" *(unser Anwesen*; also: *our property*), and with a past tense of "that which is done being" *(das Verwesene*; also: that which is decayed). We also realize that nature is all that which presents itself to us decayed from the core *(das uns ursprünglich anwest)*. We may conclude that nature is just one possibility, a kind of wind blowing at us, and that we, whatever it is we do, are digging around in that which decays, in trash, in the dirt: in short, in art. We couldn't ever decide to do that, especially since we learned in the Black Forest what was meant by "deciding," namely to come to an end, to deteriorate.

We have now adopted the following definition as a working hypothesis: "Nature is everything that occupies the natural sciences, the rest is to be called art." The upside of this definition is that if we seek to return to nature we only have to ban everything that does not belong to the natural sciences. However, we also had to acknowledge two things. First, that we owe artificial fertilizer to the natural sciences. If we only acknowledged the natural sciences, we could only permit the use of artificial fertilizer, and not natural. Second, that the natural sciences are relatively young disciplines. If we work with this definition, then nature appears to be a relatively young phenomenon—an unsettling conclusion we considered in detail:

From the beginning of humankind up to the pre-Socratic thinkers, the entire world (stones, trees, springs, clouds, rain, day and night, stars, animals, and human beings) was a context with which we could—and had to—talk. We had to pray to the phenomena, appease them, negotiate with them, that is, recognize or respect them. Ever since the pre-Socratics, however, we no longer want to recognize or acknowledge phenomena, we want to *differentiate or know* them, one after the other (first the stars, culminating in human beings). This made talking with phenomena both impossible and unnecessary (first with the stars, and in the end with human beings). This progressive trend toward differentiation and knowing, and the no-longer-having-to-recognize-or-acknowledge, represents the progress of discourse achieved in the natural sciences. Nature, therefore, is all that which we can differentiate without having to acknowledge it. From this we may conclude that nature is a subdivision of the world progressively and artificially extracted from art. We may anticipate that, over time, the entire world will belong to this subdivision. In short: Nature is to be considered the result of an artificial intervention in the world.

From the perspective of the governing party, our alarming discovery might be deemed positive. Instead of proclaiming "Back to Nature," based on the party's motto, it can advocate "Forward toward Nature." Everything that is artificial, every attempt to acknowledge anything can be vilified as reactionary. The opposition, however, could take the opportunity to turn the slogan on its head, since it demands that we advance from within art into nature artificially. It would therefore seem wise to fall back on the tradition of the dialectic, and to aver that nature is the nullification of art because of art's own internal contradiction. But now let's turn to the problem of fertilizer.

The natural sciences supply us with artificial fertilizer that facilitates superartificial natural growth, including superartificial hybrids, and therefore natural plants, thanks to the aforementioned dialectical contradiction. Because it has been differentiated and manipulated by the methods of natural science, we must concede that agriculture using artificial fertilizer is in fact natural agriculture. All so-called natural fertilization hence represents a reversion to prenatural, magical-mythical conditions. The Fundamental Green Party must therefore ban *natural* fertilization.

Assuming that the population-at-large is unable to follow our dialectical reasoning, we propose that the government again propound the slogan of our beloved fatherland: "Zip your lips!" (*Anhalt den Lippen*).

CHEMICAL INDUSTRY

A new species of insects has recently been discovered and classified. The insect is remarkable, as is the manner in which it was discovered. For *Bibliophagus convictus* stores acquired information, that is, it stores in its genetic material information that it has read (or gathered)[1] in print. The insect was found in the brain of a writer. (Should you be unfamiliar with hymenoptera in general and with Apoidea in particular, please consult the relevant encyclopedia entries in order to facilitate your understanding of the following account.)

This species rejects manuscripts and teletexts even when hungry. *Bibliophagus convictus* feeds exclusively on printed alphanumeric texts. The insect prefers entire paragraphs and chews them while its salivary glands excrete an enzyme called "criticasis," which when bonded with ink forms an acid called "informasis." The insect then rolls that mouthful, soaked with informasis, into a ball, swallows a fraction of it and passes the rest into the mouth of a member of the same species. This fellow insect repeats the process: the ball wanders from mouth to mouth until all members of the *Bibliophagus* hive have had their fill. Then they send a messenger, the *mediator,* to hand the ball on to the next hive. This creates a chain that connects all *Bibliophagus* hives. In queens, the mouthful moves from the digestive system to the ovaries, forming a connection between the informasis and the genetic material. Therefore, each consumed paragraph causes a genetic mutation within the species *Bibliophagus*. The same text twice consumed can result in redundancies (cancerous growths) in the genetic material. The risk of degeneration becomes apparent once it is recognized that consumed texts may contain quotes from those previously consumed. Hence, for Darwinian reasons, the species must intervene in the process of generating text merely to survive.

The corpse of an unknown writer was discovered not long ago. The police determined it was suicide by an unknown poison and sought to close the case; it turned out later that it was an overdose of informasis. As we know, suicide among unknown authors is quite common. The police became suspicious, however, when they came across certain anomalies and ordered an autopsy. In the writer's brain they found a *Bibliophagus,* still alive, secreting informasis. The prosecutor theorized that the insect must have penetrated the skull of its victim. He located the surgeon who had performed the trepanation. At this time, they discovered that this was far from an isolated case. Quite the contrary: an epidemic of trepanation that originated in Manhattan has advanced, via London and Paris, all the way to Frankfurt, where its current focus is at the book fair. All those performing trepanation and all those who had been trepanned refused to discuss the matter. Finally, a young theologian stepped forward. However, because he is among those who criticize ecclesiastical authority regarding questions of faith, his statement should be taken with a grain of salt.

He was reading in his bible as he does each evening. At the passage where it is written that it is not good for man to be alone [Genesis 2:18], he encountered a *Bibliophagus*. The insect used its antennae to make signs that the theologian, proficient in decoding difficult Aramaic texts, was able to interpret. They embarked on a dialogue apparently so stimulating that it made his theological fingertips drum and the insect's antennae vibrate. The dialogue (according to the theologian, nothing need be said about its contents) resulted in his decision to have the insect implanted directly into his brain so that the conversation might be more intimate.

As the investigation continued, the theologian's statements became increasingly confused. He could no longer recall who, in fact, said what, he or the *Bibliophagus*. For "Bibliophagus" he frequently substituted the word "devil." The police were forced to commit him to an institution for the mentally disturbed, and to look elsewhere for clues. One of the findings indicated that the epidemic of trepanation appeared suspiciously similar to the distribution curve of printed texts. The probability that this similarity is based on coincidence is 1:15,000. This has led to the following hypothesis: *Bibliophagus* penetrates brains to control the production of printed texts. This hypothesis is promising because it offers an explanation for why there are so many printed texts. By now there are certainly better methods for generating information, but we continue to print and write for printing presses because *Bibliophagi* sit inside the brains of writers and printers, poison them with informasis, and seduce them into producing texts so that the *Bibliophagus* species can survive. But we must acknowledge that not only authors and printers are affected, publishers, book dealers, and literary critics have been poisoned by informasis, too. We cannot otherwise explain the ongoing text inflation in what we know is an outmoded means of communication. Moreover, we must assume that informasis has a paralyzing effect on certain functions of the brain. How else can we explain why the absurdity of printing texts is so vehemently kept secret. The distribution of *Bibliophagus convictus* across human brains seems to have advanced significantly.

The controlling bodies of the chemical industry will hardly be able to stop the production of informasis by *Bibliophagi* since these bodies are likely infected themselves. We will have to accept the fact that all humans will live under the influence of this chemical substance. In other words, that all humans become executive bodies of *Bibliophagi,* and that they will compose texts that are increasingly informative and free of redundancy. (However, this wording of a chemical problem is to be read with skepticism as even this text was likely composed under the influence of *Bibliophagus*).

ANIMAL HUSBANDRY

It is highly probable, almost to the point of certainty, that humans originated from animals, a mammal that we can integrate into the family tree of animals as *Homo sapiens sapiens*. (We may derive such certainty from numerous skeletal discoveries from the Tertiary and Quaternary periods.) We must therefore deem the present nervous human (*"Homo immaterialis"*) as a type of being that was extracted from this original creature. Here, we will attempt to trace this breed stock, to reconstruct it from the fog of the past.

Animal husbandry probably commences in the twentieth century because back then reality was envisioned for the first time as a network of relationships (as a relational field), and such a worldview is a prerequisite for animal husbandry. Previously, the world appeared as a context of hard lumps (objects)—a perspective we cannot fully comprehend anymore. The primitive, "objective" world view that likely relied on the concrete experience of creatures colliding with creatures and noncreatures, that is, on an objectification of relationships, could no longer be sustained in the twentieth century. Strangely enough, it was the science of bodies, that is, physics, that first manifested the untenability of an objective worldview. In physics, the bodies proved to be relatively densely scattered regions within fields of dispersion. For example, the celestial bodies turned out to be dense scatterings (protrusions, curvatures) in the gravitational field, and the hydrogen atom turned out to be a compaction (groove) in crisscrossing fields of the "strong" and the "weak" force and of electromagnetism. As a result, the objects turned out to be agglomerations of energy, and matter concentrated energy. It was also technically possible to dissolve matter into energy and to concentrate energy into matter. This discovery forced the elimination of the primitive ideological concept *object* in other areas as well. A few examples will suffice to demonstrate:

Biology (the science of creatures and greenstuff) always contended that its task was to examine organisms (living bodies) as representing biological reality. Then it recognized protrusions (epiphenomena) from the biomass in these organisms, which is to be considered as a field of relations that transmits genetic information. At the same time, it recognized that the organisms themselves function within relational fields (ecosystems) and are not to be considered individual bodies. That allowed for the biomass to be manipulated (to synthesize previously nonexistent organisms from the genetic information), to produce identical organisms (clones), and to program previously nonexistent ecosystems.

Neurophysiology freed itself from the obligation to localize some kind of thought-, sensory-, or decision-making centers in the nervous system (and especially in the brain), and it recognized in the nervous system a relational field in which information (data) gets processed into feelings, thoughts, desires, and decisions. That allowed not only for the disciplined control of mental processes (for example by means of electrodes in the brain), but also and especially for the production of types of artificial intelligence.

Psychology, which long believed that it was dealing with individual psyches, began to discover that the "I" (or "self" or "identity") is to be viewed as the tip of an iceberg that is constructed out of collective psychic processes, that is, from processes that are transspecific and relate to all living creatures, and not just the human species. It thus recognized in the human "I" (in the "subject") an epiphenomenal protrusion from a universal field of psychic relations.

Philosophy began to liberate itself from "eternal" problems that had emerged by necessity from the ideology of the "object," on the one hand, and the human "subject," on the other, and it recognized in object and subject extrapolated abstractions from the concrete field of relations that Husserl called the *lifeworld (Lebenswelt)*. This facilitated a philosophical perspective of looking closely at the "things themselves," that is, looking at the network of relationships.

Once the ideology of objects and bodies had made way for a perspective of fields, it became possible to deal with animal husbandry. It was clear from the outset that the human body (this creaturely protrusion from the biomass) is badly constructed (consider disease, pain, death; consider also the limitations of the physical senses and of brain competency). Equally obvious was the fact that one could not be freed from the contingency of the environment as long as the body is dependent on the environment (consider nutrition, clothing), and that it would be a fallacy to expect freedom by manipulating the environment. And it also became obvious that all involvement with "culture" (e.g., storing, processing, and distributing acquired information) is brought into question by the body because acquired information cannot be biologically inherited. Therefore, the decision was soon made to shed the body and become removed from that which is animal, in particular because machines had already taken on most bodily functions anyway, and most experiences (from imagination to orgasm) could be simulated without mediation by the body (for example, by drugs).

A significant challenge was the shedding of individuality, this "I-core," once considered solid and called the soul. Clinging to this corporeal remnant seemed prudent (for reasons unclear today), even though existential analysis had already demonstrated that the "I" is that node in the social network which we address with "you" (because you can only identify yourself in relation to others), and even though telematic technology had already analyzed this interconnectedness. But, in the end, this "self"-ideology was left behind as well, and animal husbandry was under way. Now things appear as follows:

A network of nerve fibers surrounds the Earth and Mars. It swims in a nutrient solution, constantly synthesizing new information in its synapses. And we are the undulations of the network swaying in harmony: nervous humans, *Homines immateriales*—movements of love bred from animals.

PART III

SCENES FROM POLITICS

WAR

The future consequences of war had been correctly predicted in the 1980s: 3 billion dead; radical changes in climate; the destruction of a considerable part of material culture and of sociopolitical structures; vast numbers of plant, animal, and human mutations. It seems that the prewar state was considered valuable because, surprisingly, the consequences of war were deemed negative ("collective suicide"). Surprising because a great many voices considered the prewar state ruinous and unsustainable ("This cannot go on!"). The details:

Three billion dead: At the time, it was determined in unison that there were too many people. The elderly could no longer be fed in the developed areas, the underdeveloped areas were teeming with children who could not be nourished. All peaceful methods to control the demographic explosion (the pill, abortion, traffic accidents, drugs, AIDS, and so forth) had been ineffective. The overcrowding of schools led to a deterioration in the level of intellect. Illiterates populated the universities. All public spaces such as streets, beaches, and ski slopes were saturated with masses of people. The world was seething with people who were alien to each other but forced to come into physical contact. The individual lived embattled, in fear, and lonely within the crowds. Demographic projections forecast a veritably infernal massification. Death by mutual smothering. Nonetheless, nuclear explosion was rated negatively compared with a demographic solution to the problem—as if mass death, that is, death together with all one's loved ones, would be worse than what was deemed necessary to experience the death of a loved one from cancer, a circulatory disorder, or asphyxiation. In short, from all the causes that we understand to be a "natural death."

Climate change: Before the war, a large portion of the available water mass was stored in the form of ice around the poles. Back then, they were concerned that an ice melt could increase the sea level, resulting in potential flooding of port cities. Remarkably, they did not foresee the irrigation of the desert, the climatic equilibrium of the earth, the radiant morning following a nuclear night, the eternal spring following a nuclear winter. This blindness may be attributed, not least, to the fear mentioned earlier.

Material destruction: Back then, increasing automation and rationalization led to an oversaturation of the environment with useless stuff. People could no longer find a way toward each other or toward nature. All methods to stem this environmental pollution—such as by planning, economic crises, or increased consumption—had failed. Despite that, out of a lack of the imagination or creative foresight, no one seems to have advocated for the nuclear destruction of this stuff. The beauty of the ruins—if we think of the World Trade Center or the Detroit automobile plants, now covered with lush vegetation—was unimaginable back then.

Collapse of structures: Even though structures such as family, class, the people, and the state were deemed obsolete and harmful at the time—and they were indeed in a state of slow decay—and even though precursors of the current monastic order of society (kibbutzim, ashrams, oases in the American desert, alternative groups) already existed, they apparently did not realize that the old, mummified (and thus air-polluting) structures could only be completely abolished in favor of the new structure with the help of thermonuclear intervention.

Mutations: At the time, they believed in ecologically impossible monsters such as giant insects, meat-eating plants, and disfigured idiots, because mutations triggered by radioactivity had been labeled pathological cases, even though, first of all, the mechanism of natural selection was quite well known and, second, they should have been aware that the radioactivity released during the war accelerates the process of creating superior species. For that reason, they could not predict the rich branching of ecosystems today, their variety and abundance, and certainly not the refinement of the human being.

The contradiction between the correctly calculated prediction of the future and inadequately intuited foresight can be traced back to an insufficiently developed theory of catastrophes. *Catastrophe* meant a point on a projected curve from where it was impossible to calculate the curve's future trajectory—this much was clear even then. However, they considered this point to be dangerous, not the emergence of something new. Because everything unknown is terrible, they feared catastrophes—instead of inducing them intentionally, as we do.

The reasons for visualizing the now no-longer-comprehensible primitive fear of catastrophes that was common in prewar times are pedagogical. Because we are currently observing symptoms that signal a relapse into prewar mentalities. Our almost paradisiacal situation seems to elicit mental inertia. Numerous monastic communities seem to value keeping what has been created rather than repeatedly questioning all that has been accomplished. Death-defying courage and an openness to adventure, both of which we owe to war, are beginning to slacken. Hence a warning: if we don't resist the looming inertia, an inertia that was generally called *progress* in prewar times, we will relapse into a prewar state. And that is calculable in advance because inertia is calculable.

AURAL OBEDIENCE

Do not expect any groundbreaking insights from my essay, beyond those by acousticians, phoneticians, and musicians. I am hard of hearing and can only tell you about my hearing aid (Hörapparat). Please forgive me for shouting at you. I do this so that I may better hear myself. I submit that I can see better since I have had the hearing aid. Now sounds reach me and I look in their direction. For example, I've never paid attention to hydraulic drills as closely as I do now because I can hear them. Thinking that hearing and seeing are opposite modes of perception is a widespread error. It's like thinking that the Greeks had worse hearing than the Jews because they saw more deeply, or the Jews had worse eyesight than the Greeks because they obeyed the call. Or that Homer was blind because he listened to the voice of the muse, and the great seers were deaf to the sounds of everyday life. Quite the contrary: the better your hearing, the better you see. Only those who hear the voice of the daemon can theorize.

Hearing aids are powered by batteries that go on strike from time to time. At those times, you hear only a hum. It is the voice of flowing blood (which the Nazis amplified). But batteries have the advantage that, unlike blood, they can be turned off. Hearing aids are not only glasses, but eyelids as well. They allow us to shut our ears, creating a private silence. Hearing, more so than eyesight (Gesicht), is political. Instead of political views (Ansicht), we need to speak of political aural obedience. Voting is political engagement, the harmonizing of the "voices of the people," (the low spheres in harmony with the high spheres) thanks to polyphony or thanks to monotony (elimination of the higher spheres and elevation of the "basso continuo" as the carrying voice). All of this creates noise; "pianissimo" has no place in any political program, and if it did, it would be unheard of. Hearing aids that you can turn off are devices enabling periodic politicization and depoliticization. And switching off the apparatus is no head-in-the-sand politics; it is consciously antipolitical. Hearing aids are devices for freedom.

It is not true that we open and close our eyes volitionally. Some blinking is involuntary, and you never know for sure whether it is, in fact, a sign of conspiracy or just a tic. Our eyelids not only criticize the political scene, they are also involuntary reflexes of this scene. This is not the case with hearing aids. They are not "natural" like eyelids; they are cultural, "artificial." Switching them off represents a devastating critique of proclamations. Here, the "nature/culture" dialectic comes into play. Hearing aids were produced as analogues of eyelids, but we can learn to manipulate our eyelids like hearing aids. Thanks to hearing aids, we can see better, we can switch our views (Ansichten) on and off. Hearing aids not only permit us to go about our vocations better than the Jews, but also to elaborate theories better than the Greeks. For example, they enable us to create cameras (Fotoapparate), that is, eyes that blink like hearing aids. We do not know whether Daguerre or Niépce were hard of hearing.

One further remark: if you listen closely to the world, you detect not white noise but an orchestral vibration. A programmed noise. It is as if a sound filter had been turned on between yourself and the world. A hearing aid, to be exact. The uncomfortable and intolerable aspect of this apparatus is its invisibility. You are, if I may say, blind to your own hearing aids. I, however, can see mine. Not only can I see them, I can see through them. I know who programmed them—a Japanese company. But you are blind to the programming apparatus (and therefore deaf). For this reason, you need to listen when others tell you something (like the aged Kant, who was probably also hard of hearing) about "forms of perception," which are famously categorical like imperatives. Allow me to scream this at you: you are servile (*hörig*), equipped with nontransparent hearing aids.

I warned you not to expect too much from my views on hearing. I cannot offer you a method for political fine-tuning or private silence. I am just as shortsighted as you are because I am not deaf enough to see further. I am just as "dumb" as you, to the extent that "dumb" and "deaf" are synonyms. Among us "dumb dunces": whenever we think to listen up (*aufhorchen*), we only obey (*gehorchen*) new, equally programmed provocations. This is how things are with our wrongly celebrated human freedom. Nonetheless, I hope I have made a small contribution to our symposium on "The World of Notes and Sounds." As someone who is hard of hearing, I shout at you: "Please take a look at the hearing aids that you walk around with, so that you may see a bit further and listen a bit more closely. So that you may stop obeying."

PERPETUAL PEACE

Just leave us in peace with your eternal processes. The resting state[1] we have assumed is a position. It is placeless (utopian) and thus represents an abundance of time. We have achieved the resting state because we were able to synchronize all places and remove them from the world. Everything has become simultaneous and spaceless. All possibilities have moved to the present as all places have been reduced to one single point, to the *here* and *now*. They have become real. And we, too, as we find ourselves in a resting state, have pulled out of the flow of time and have become completely realized beings. We have achieved the goal of history—and not only of this one history, but, generally, of all kinds of histories. At this position and all around it, all kinds of possibilities are fulfilled. We can observe this fulfillment from our position. With our tranquility satisfied *(befriedigt)*, we are pleased *(zufrieden)*. This is perpetual peace.

We should contemplate the incisive comment by the previous speaker that peace is a condition, and wherever we find movement, there is war. He probably meant that, first, all peace movements are aggressive endeavors and, second, that pacifism and imperialism are synonymous—as suggested by the term "pax romana." Conversely, he probably also meant that all movements (all aggressive endeavors) are to be considered pacific because they pursue a kind of peace whose motto is *si vis pacem pare bellum* [if you want peace, prepare for war], which pretty much summarizes all historical acts.

Peace is a manifestation of old age. Only those at rest are responsible for peace. Peace manifests when time gets old, and it manifests when society gets old. Peace is senility. When time was young, it was in flux (läufig). In fact, it was simultaneously preliminary (vorläufig) and incidental (beiläufig). It kept society up to date (auf dem laufenden). It constantly bore young. Ever since the pre-Socratics, many people have racked their brains over this. Some have suggested that time carries all things as it courses. Others have suggested that all things are born through and with time, that the course of time (war) is the father of all things (polemos pater panton). Yet others have suggested that the essence ("to on") remains untouched by the course of time. Most everyone agrees, however, that time is running toward a goal, toward a dam, toward a "fullness of time," in short, toward perpetual peace. People who were still up-to-date thought that perpetual peace was a state in which everything was fulfilled, in which humanity faces fulfillment tranquilly. Today we know that the fullness of time has not been achieved. It is exhausted. We do not perceive ourselves as in some kind of beyond; we perceive ourselves as in something concrete. Perpetual peace comes about when everything, exhausted, has concentrated on the *here* and *now*.

We have accomplished peace with the help of a certain technique called telematics. This technique allowed us to make all places present such that all events around the world appear to us simultaneously. The simultaneity of all events has resulted in all of them becoming meaningless. And the fact that the events appear to us on screens, for example, has resulted in all of them becoming noninteractional. The meaninglessness and abstractness of all events is exactly what has facilitated this apathy, the kind of *vita contemplativa* we live in this resting state. Telematics is the technique of fulfillment. It is fulfillment itself.

Telematics fulfills what was promised from the beginning, for example, the promise of the eternal peace of the Sabbath, from which humanity emerges from the flow of time to contemplate eternity. Or the platonic promise of a tranquil (theoretical) life that permits the recognition of perpetual forms. Or the promise of the stoa, that is, to ascend from the suffering of the transient into eternity, thanks to equanimity and insensitivity (ataraxia and apathy). However, telematics represents not only the fulfillment of Western promises, but also of Buddhist ones—not surprising, given its partially Japanese origins.

Telematics, of course, is not the first attempt to achieve perpetual peace by technological means. Its predecessor is film. Back then, the course of time was fed onto celluloid strips, which were cut and glued, accelerated and decelerated such that it was possible to view the beginning and end of time simultaneously. One was above the times such that they could be programmed. But this was not yet true peace. The producer was dependent on actors (troublemakers). We have only been able to speak of the factual indifference and abstractness of all events and of the end of history, since telematics stored the course of time immaterially and made it retrievable (and revocable) at the push of a button. It is therefore not enough to ascend from the flow of time and survey it in order to gain peace. One has to be able to make time as well.

As long as we were kept informed, we thought, mistakenly, that while being in the flow of time, we could make history within history. Only now that we are detached because history is indifferent and meaningless to us do we recognize that it is only possible to do anything while being in a state of *dégagement*, indifferent and contemplative. To produce means to pull upward—which is why producers need to be above matters, to pull them toward themselves (retrieve). Telematics permits us to retrieve history, to make it present at the push of a button, and also to make it disappear again with another push of the button. We find ourselves in a new condition that permits us to combine and generate all kinds of courses of history to create new ones, even those we invent ourselves. Quietly and deliberately we can compose ever-new histories in this condition, that is, we can make history in the true sense of the word. The resting state is the position of God.

The difference between a person who stays up-to-date and someone who faces the course of time while at rest is the difference between an actor and a player. Whoever stays up-to-date will be carried away by the course of time and cannot achieve peace. Something happens around him constantly, and by default he is a dealer, an actor, an *agonist*. He presents the protagonist in his own agony and the antagonist of the agonies of all other victims carried along in the course of time. A person who faces the flow of time, however, does not perceive things as objects that resist him, but as envisioned possibilities. He can play with them, move and set them just like chess pieces or Go stones in order to create new circumstances that never existed before. Things don't slip between his fingers anymore (there is no more *becoming*); they are available to him at all times (stored in a memory that can be manipulated). There is no more flow of time; according to the program, everything is centered on the person who deliberates. Only in the fullness of time, and from within same fullness, does making history become possible. Only at the end of history is it possible to create *res gestae*, to create a historical act.

The difference between the person engaged and within the flow of time *(Homo faber)* and the person at rest, contemplating *(Homo ludens)*, is the difference between the dealer and the artist. It is evident that the dealer acts in accordance with the program of the artist. The artist proves to be the dramaturge of the drama History, and the dealer proves to be his chess piece, his puppet. We total artists at rest, we, the programmers of all dramas and agonies, paradoxically represent the source of all acts. We are the *unmoved movers*, the motors behind all motives.

This, then, is perpetual peace: to program all action and, along with it, all suffering—indifferently and with sovereign apathy to contemplate it with satisfaction. Perpetual peace is not human, it is superhuman. And that is why those who are still up-to-date, those who are still human, call up to us to say: *"requiescant in pacem"*—rest in peace.

REVOLUTION

Not too long ago, when I welcomed you to Three Powers Square, I called out to you, "Allah is Brazilian!" My Arabic may still be rusty, as you have noticed, but my faith is all the firmer for it. My fraternal friend Muhammad Omar, president of the United States, correctly observed that the essence of Islam is humility. I will therefore gladly renounce my arrogant triumphalism. The world revolution that began in Atlanta, Georgia, in 1991 should really not be considered complete, despite its glorious victories. It is not seriously threatened from the outside, and the counterrevolutionary groups smoldering in various marginal areas will, Allah permitting, be snuffed out. But as is becoming apparent here, at the First Congress of the Umma in Brasilia, internal disputes threaten to tear the revolution apart.

Typically enough, the threat emerges from Uzbekistan, a situation that makes clear the problem that must be resolved. In brief: the Caliphate is in danger of splitting into a Western half (Maghreb) and an Eastern one (Mizr). I know very well that my explanation is much too simplistic to be accepted by the theoreticians and scholars in attendance. At issue is not, as these gentlemen will rightly argue, a geographical split, but an ideological one, a contradiction between knowledge *(Erkenntnis)* and values. These intellectual perspectives are not subject to geographical limits. And, indeed, adherents of these two tendencies may be found everywhere. The most recent elections have shown that, proportionally, more people voted for the Bukhara Party in North America than in China.

Nonetheless, I insist on my simplification, thereby invoking historical experience.

At the core of the dispute that has been voiced so ferociously here is the question whether the teachings of the Prophet are to be interpreted politically or theologically. No one doubts that the two interpretations complement each other and must ultimately coincide. The question is, which interpretation is to be given precedence. As we now know, this question is a matter of life and death. From a political perspective, the goal of Islam is to build a universal, economically and socially just society that overcomes all racial prejudice, and in which it is possible for each Muslim to serve God. From a theological perspective, it is the goal of Islam to guide each individual human being to God with the help of daily and nightly prayer and, spontaneously, to make him a member of a society in which God is personified on earth. The political interpretation calls for rather different measures than the theological one. It turns out that both measures cannot be acted on simultaneously.

Although both interpretations are contained in the Quran, they represent two divergent mentalities. One could call them political praxis and theological theory. Simplifying a bit, we find that the practical mentality evolved primarily in the Confucian East, the theoretical one in the infidel, primarily Christian West. Although Islam is a synthesis of both these mentalities, elevating the two forms of faithlessness to the level of True Faith (and please do not accuse me of regressing into Marxism, this fool of Islam, when I express this); and although Islam cancels out this contradiction, the two mentalities are nullified within it and contradict each other for precisely this reason. We are dealing here with facts repeatedly proven in history: the split in Christianity into Orthodoxy and Catholicism, the split in Islam into Shiite and Sunni, the split in the Mongolian empires, the split in Marxism into the Soviet Union and China.

Regarding the contradiction between theory and praxis, we should note that theoretical thinking leads to the application of theorems, that is, to technology, a powerful praxis. Additionally, practical thinking leads to strategies, which are powerful paratheoretical points of view. This explains why the West was able to conquer the globe in the nineteenth century, and why, in the twentieth, the East was able to seize power. Theoretical thinking in no way occupies a level different from practical thinking. Both forms must eventually collide. Unfortunately, we are currently observing how this murderous clash takes place within the Caliphate itself. We are in the process of attacking each other.

The Bukhara ideology is basically a renaissance of practical Eastern (Chinese-Mongolian) thought and action. The kind of Jihad that is currently being waged under the banner of this ideology is, essentially, an invasion of the Western theoretical world supported by computer science and electronics, and carried out by strategists of the likes of Genghis and Kublai Khan. True, their battle cries call for the "Equality of all races!" and "Equal distribution of all goods!" But fundamentally their goal is to wipe out Whites and Blacks, that is, the minority. In view of the fact that we have Black Muslims to thank for the revolution, there is a danger that they will not only devour their own children, but also their own fathers.

It seems to me that the answer to this challenge is not to insist on the theological, theoretical interpretation of the Prophet's message so as to get killed while lost in prayer. We must accept the risk of splitting the Caliphate, and grab the sword ourselves. Such a split is not fatal for Islam; it is in the spirit of its mission. That mission is not the victory of the revolution, but permanent revolution. As a good Muslim and mufti, as well as in my capacity as a Mulatto, I appeal to the Maghreb to confront the Bukharists so that Islam does not peter out in practical and political, murderous barbarisms.

A shot is fired. The Brazilian president collapses to the floor. The delegates assembled in the hall strangle each other.

PARLIAMENTARY DEMOCRACY

The last communications that refer to parliamentary democracy (literally: people's power talked to pieces) stem from the twenty-third century and are contained in a document called the *Pedifesto,* found in the Ulan Bator archives. This document helps us to reconstruct this peculiar institution. The purpose of parliamentary democracy seems to have been to relieve people of all responsibility for political decisions. The method was called *elections*—a process by which the people periodically and voluntarily transferred all political freedom of choice to a small select group. Elections existed to pick such a small group out of a bigger one, consisting of *candidates* (more or less literally: people with clean vests). In order to organize and pre-program this selection, there were strange organizations called *political parties.* Let's take a closer look at the aforementioned document.

The *Pedifesto* originated in the year 2287. The general situation was as follows: the transfer of floral and faunal life into the oceans was practically finished, but the continents were still overcrowded because the population of the planets had not yet begun. Genetic surgery on humans was supposed to help relieve this pressing problem. Strangely enough, the first step was to replace the legs, which had become superfluous, with wheeled extremities. This was probably done in the hope that greater mobility would lead to better dispersion of humanity. However, the loss of two legs and feet was felt to be humiliating.

Two parties emerged. One party took the position that one should, despite difficulties, insist on the perpetuation of feet. This party was called "Root and Dignity Party" (*Wurzel-und-Würde, Weh-Weh*, lit. booboo). This party wrote the *Pedifesto*. The other party took the position that feet could be retained—but only if people were prepared to assume the costs of populating other planets (Mars foremost among them). This party was called the "Up-and-Out-Party" (*Hinan-und-Hinaus, Ha-Ha*). From the *Pedifesto,* we know that the latter won the election. The title *Pedifesto* makes sense when we recall an older document that is no longer extant, the *Communist Manifesto*. This lost but oft-cited document appears to have taken the position that a human being must use his hands—as he reaches into things, as he handles and understands them—in order to overcome his conditioning by things. The word "manifesto" expresses the importance of hands. The *Pedifesto* should be understood as a continuation and upending of the *Communist Manifesto*. It states that humans are rooted in the earth with their feet ("earth" means ground as well as planet), and that they will lose their human dignity if they lose their grounding *(bodenlos)*. In order to understand the civil war that broke out after the *Pedifesto,* however, we must bring up another category of parliamentary democracy, namely, "Right" (emphasis on the unchanging) and "Left" (emphasis on the changeable).

The *Communist Manifesto* was Left because it emphasized the changes in the material world brought about by hands. Conversely, the *Pedifesto* was Right because it emphasized the presumably unchangeable rootedness (down-to-earth quality) of the human being. It was immediately clear that this categorization was imprecise and primitive. The changes that have been achieved are based on the assumption that hands are an unchangeable given. In this respect, the *Manifesto* should be considered to be on the Right. The *Pedifesto* is based on the assumption that the human being can come unstuck from the ground. In this respect, it should be considered on the Left. What we learn from the available documents, in fact, is that all parties on the Left eventually came to be Right, especially when they were able to seize political power, and that all parties on the Right were originally Left. Since election campaigns were confrontations between

Right and Left candidates, this primitivism and illogic of the category "Right/Left" is indispensable for understanding parliamentary democracy and its catastrophic demise.

Studying the *Pedifesto* reveals something else. There is another word for parliamentary democracy, namely *demagogy* (people's chatter). Back then the former was used melioratively, the latter pejoratively; however, the *Pedifesto* shows that they are synonyms. A mocking "Ha-Ha" directed at the opposition party can clearly be heard emanating from the *Pedifesto*. It is the response to the cries of Boo-Boo resounding from the opposition party. *Democratic debate,* sometimes also termed *freedom of speech,* consisted mainly of Ha-Ha and Boo-Boo sounds broadcast by the media. These sounds pulverized all information about the overcrowding of the continents. The problem in need of resolution fell into oblivion, and the parties fought each other with meaningless words (slogans, *Schlagwort*).

As we know, in 2295, these words were replaced by nuclear weapons. The problem of overcrowding was resolved. After the continents were redeveloped and repopulated, and after the planets had been colonized, all political decisions came to be made by means of computation of all individual choices. However, since the end of the twentieth century, parliamentary democracy and demagogy had, at least technically, become obsolete. As early as 1968 a "Leftist" is known to have said, arguably based on the *Communist Manifesto,* "If we didn't have computers we would have to invent them for the council constitution." The method for feeding all individual choices into central computers was fully developed and available by 2287. The civil war, with all its indescribable suffering, could thus have been prevented. But this is thinking nonhistorically, because in order to replace parliamentary democracy with computation we had to redefine the concept of freedom. However, that was possible only after the civil war.

ARYAN IMPERIALISM

Report from the Department of Counterintelligence to the Prime Minister: Shalom. Our agent was received by the King of all Aryans and Non-Aryans in Shahr-e-Zabul on Lake Hamun. Darius was sitting on the Peacock Throne, at his feet the tail-eating snake Ourubo- ros, and the Twelve Satraps—among them Khomeini and Dr. Kissinger—stood on both sides in hierarchical order. Visible on the large screen behind His Majesty's back was a digital map of Earth. At the center of the projection was Jerusalem, which was, however, indi- cated by its ancient name, Ari-El (the Master's lion), and from which continents and oceans seemed to radiate. The Earth was circular and red; at its center—in gold—the territory of the Persian Empire in the year 490 BC, and identified as "Aryan Manda." Jerusalem was at the margin of the Empire such that the Empire itself was off-center. It skewed to the East. There were three figures at the center of the Empire: a woman bearing the nameplate "Esther Ishtar," to her right a man bearing the nameplate "Ahasver Xerxes," and to her left a rabbi bearing the nameplate "Mordechai Marduk." A fiery inscription hov- ered above the three figures read "Mene, mene, tekel upharsin."

Benevolently, the King received our agent with the words: "Should I forget you, oh Jerusalem, oh then my right arm shall wither." Then he pressed one of the buttons he had within reach, and the map of Earth vanished, giving way to a scene from the Iran–Iraq war. He pressed a button again and a Mercator projection appeared, on which the Pamir Plateau was shown in relief in gold. From there blotches of color spread out across the map: yellow ones into the East, blue ones toward the South, and green ones into the West. When the Earth was covered with them an inscription arose from the Plateau of Pamir, "Ahura Mazda." At once, the entire map turned golden. At the same time, as if on a palimpsest, the letters JHVH appeared between those of the inscription to yield an illegible and therefore unpronounceable word. The satraps fell to the ground.

The King rose to speak and explained to our agent: "You just now witnessed the history of humanity. When we, the Aryans, broke out from the roof of the world to aid the light in its victory over the night, we were inspired by the spirit of dialectics. The Aryan word for divine is DV. But it not only means *deus,* but also 'two' *(zwei)* and, therefore, 'doubt' *(Zweifel).* It was clear to us that the light can only prevail if it overcomes the dark within itself. In our radiant advance against the powers of Satan, we came across you, JHVH. As you well know, this unpronounceable and unimaginable name signifies *hayah* (it was), *hove* (it is), and *ehyeh* (it will be). Being reveals itself in this name as indivisible and singular *(JHVH echad)* and does not equate with the Aryan term DV. My predecessors, Darius and Cyrus, tried to incorporate JHVH, and it almost worked under Xerxes the Great. But the attempt had to fail. Since then, we Aryans have kept trying to eliminate you Jews.

"As you have seen, we have been successful in subjugating all of humanity in a dialectical battle. Our great Satrap, Gautama the Enlightened, conquered the East in the name of Ahuras and broke through the darkness of delusional entanglement (Maya). In the heartland of our Empire, in India, we opened a path for the light with the help of our holy books, the Vedas. In the West, we created science and the resulting technology by using the dialectic method to help the light of reason triumph over the Satanic powers of ignorance and superstition. These three seemingly divergent advances of light over dark, the paths of Buddhism, of Hinduism, and of Western science, have always been connected, openly or surreptitiously. Our throne has always been the focal point from which Aryan inspiration fed strength and hope into the three avatars of Aryan wisdom. And yet, none of my predecessors have won a final victory against the darkness.

"At fault is our inability to integrate your JHVH into our Aryan philosophical tradition, and then to eliminate Him from it. Like an indigestible chunk, or rather, like a glowing ember, JHVH is stuck in our throats. He cannot be swallowed, nor can He be spit out. You may believe me—and you know it to be true—when I describe my predecessors' efforts to find a solution. I need only mention the kind of thought gymnastics practiced by Dostoevsky and Nietzsche, and I won't even touch on primitive approaches to the problem such as pogroms and gas ovens. But I also believe that you have difficulty in dealing with us. I have studied your Cabbalistic literature and cannot avoid the thought that you are condemned to fail just like we are. Unless we combine forces.

"That is why I have decided to adopt the policies of my predecessors from the fifth century BC, that is, to begin diplomatic relations with you and, together, finally succeed in building the Empire. As you know, back then, my predecessors supported the construction of your Second Temple, and your prophet Daniel predicted our final victory (upharsin). That is why I have asked your government to have you come for a visit. At the same time, I ordered my two Satraps, the Ayatollah and the Doctor, to take necessary measures on my behalf. Accordingly, the current war between the Iranian rump state and the Satanic powers is to be considered a first step toward a collaboration between me and you.

"So, this is the message that I ask you to please deliver to your government: Israel should enter into a secret alliance with Iran to prepare a definitive synthesis between Ahura and JHVH. This shall clear a path toward an Aryan World Empire, toward the victory of light. If, contrary to expectation, your government should reject this suggestion, then I will be forced to initiate a final solution to this problem."

Such is our report. We expect the Prime Minister to inform us whether we may maintain contact with Shahr-e-Zabul, or whether we should initiate something to counter this neo-Nazism.

BLACK IS BEAUTIFUL

Dakar is the wrong place to discuss a theory of color, because theory requires a distancing from the object. But here we are not able to take this step away from color. For us, color is exactly what we are up against. If we distance ourselves from it, we risk losing ourselves. Nonetheless, I plan to present to the Troisième Congrès International de la Négritude a few theoretical ideas about color, convinced that only when People of Color work out a theory of color does the problem of color truly gain a voice.

Based on an extremely dubious taxonomy, humanity is divided into three categories of color: 57 percent yellow, 36 percent white, and 7 percent black. This taxonomy is doubtful not only because it is uncomfortable, but also because it is based on a faulty understanding of color. We may disregard the fact that it is uncomfortable. It is true that there is hardly a human being who neatly fits into any of these three categories. Since categories are always theoretical, however, you can force the phenomenon to adapt to them. For example, red skins can theoretically be classified as yellow (mutated Mongols), and brown people theoretically as a mixture of yellow, black, and white people. What defeats this taxonomy is not the fact that it is completely use-less, but that it is theoretically wrong. White and black are not colors. If the majority of humanity, in its core, is indeed yellow (and this is undoubtedly the case, since it accords with all theories of color), then it would be expected that humanity tends either toward red or toward purple. But there are no green mulattos. Down with racism!

I allowed myself to get carried away by nontheoretical considerations, but I have regained my distance so that I can address the problem of white and black with composure. If the word "color" means a visible portion of the field of light oscillations, then *white* is not a color, because it is not perceived as a visible portion, but as a sum of all rays. For a parallel reason, *black,* too, is not a color, because the eye perceives it as a complete absence of these rays—and, rather importantly, as overridden rays. If one switches perspectives on this problem, one could say: if a surface reflects all incoming light rays, then it is white; if it absorbs them all, it is black; if it absorbs them only partially, then it appears colored. You will have noted my efforts to formulate these definitions without any engagement and with the requisite scientific dispassion.

Every phenomenological observation of all Black cultures proves the correctness of color theory. Such cultures are open to light, absorb it. The incomparable rhythm everything in us oscillates is nothing but sublimated oscillation of light within ourselves. We, the Black people, are the real children of light—of the sun, the moon and the stars—especially because we swallow the light, save it within ourselves, and override it as culture. To date, we have not, however, drawn the proper radical conclusions from this theoretical perspective on color. Our encounter today should give us the courage to formulate our message clearly and then to act accordingly.

Based on the (questionable) taxonomy mentioned above, 57 percent of people are *yellow* (colored), that is, such people only absorb part of the incident light. They represent a mass that is indifferent to light, which is what the natural development of the human species entails—because yellow is probably the natural color of humanity. Thirty-six percent of humanity is white, shuts itself off to light, pushes away all light, and rejects all that is radiant. It is probably the cadaverous aspect of white people that is to blame for this rejection, which, in truth, results from a rejection of life. Only a small fraction of humanity, an elite of 7 percent, is black, hospitable to light, permeated by it and determined to swallow it. Philanthropy, properly understood, would happen if the Black elite finally decided to stir the rest of humanity and to move it into the oscillation of light. Philanthropy, properly understood, would be anthropophagy, which would help us to imbibe the rest of humanity in order to turn it *black*.

It is a historical fact that, over the past centuries, the white minority seized power and subjugated the yellow and black majority. It was probably able to do so because it reflects the light, negating both light and life, something often described using the euphemisms "science" and "technology." We have had plenty opportunity over the past centuries to experience the deadliness of these white reflections on our own bodies. If, therefore, anthropophagy is the kind of philanthropy characteristic of us, then, based on my ideas about color theory, we should begin with the systematic devouring of whites.[1] The remaining issue of the great yellow mass can be left for a distant future.

The strategy presented here rests on straightforward ideas about color theory. But it has an aesthetic side as well. Compared to the bland yellowness of the great mass and the disgusting corpse-whiteness of those still in power, the radiant blackness of the human elite is beautiful. I invite you to take on the burden of beauty (Black Man's burden).

PART IV

SHOWDOWN

A BREATHER

We have looked both individually and together at the twenty-first scenario (which examines blackness) and the seventeenth (which looks at peace). We then asked the programmer of the imagination[1] to incorporate our viewpoints into the series. We differ with regard to the Blackness of peace, but we are seeking a congruence of both views. Our names, that of my colleague, Job, and my own, Ulysses, are, we think, not entirely unknown to you. This knowledge will facilitate the decipherment of the image projected here.

From my point of view, the resting state, this all-devouring black hole, is to be considered a deep, but not abysmal, wave trough within the web of phenomena. We all are swimming in the surges of events that lift us up and push us down. We must part the wave surges with our arms to get anywhere. We are not aware of where we wish to go, but we are driven by an inner urge to be homeward bound. This urge we call the love of wisdom or, in short, philosophy. However, this urge is not all that propels us forward; the surges themselves seem to move in a certain direction. We want to go where the surges take us. When we love wisdom, we love fate. That is the real difference between a philosopher and a hero, that is, between the futurologist and the terrorist presented in the first scenario. The hero fights against fate and is devoured by the surge. The philosopher desires fate, and will therefore advance up to the black hole, achieve a state of rest, and with it, peace.

There is a net in the black hole, I call it *topos uranikos* (heaven, paradise). All surges of phenomena, everything that has ever happened, are captured in its loops and held for all times. We call these loops *eideiai* (forms). But the net is not apparent to those swimming in the surges because it is black. It does not appear. Nonetheless, there is one perspective from which it becomes visible. We call it *theoria*. The net comes into view through this theoretical perspective as an orderly network or web. We call this order *logic*. Therefore, the black hole emerges as an ordered network, invisible from the perspective of the swimmers, but that captures the disorderly surges of the visible, apparent web in its forms. Everything that happens is formalized in the black hole, reduced to its forms. Apparent and seeming phenomena are unveiled therein, that is, preserved: they become truth. Whoever has advanced into the black hole ceases to get lost in the surges of waves, and emerges from error into truth. He may contemplate the eternal, true forms forever. He lives in the eternal peace of truth, of the beautiful and the good.

My colleague has a different view of the black hole, or, rather, he does not see it, he hears it. To him, the black hole is a voice that quietly invites him to break out of the absurd racket, this noisy pile of shards upon which he sits and scrapes himself, and to dust himself off. The voice is barely audible for all the clatter of shards. Only those with excellent hearing—my colleague calls it "faith"—can detect it. This voice will become a profession and calling, and he will try to follow it. According to my colleague, it will lead him "onto the path of righteousness," and to the black hole. In his language, the hole is called the "Sabbath." During the Sabbath there is eternal silence, all singing and recitation have been quieted. That's why we don't speak of the black hole. My colleague thinks that the Greek word *theologia* (in German approximately: "speaking of the black hole") is a self-contradiction.

Although one must remain silent about the black hole and not even speak its name, we must nonetheless speak of the journey to it. My colleague agrees with me when I think of this journey as love. But he does not understand it in the sense of the love of wisdom. He thinks of it as the love of the other. When he says "the other," he has in mind all other human beings, and especially those who are neighbors, but apart from that he thinks of those who are Very Other. One can only achieve the peace of the Sabbath if one loves one's neighbor more than anything else and, through him, the Very Other. His interpretation is as follows: as long as we love things—I would say, as long as we are lost in appearance—we must suffer because these things are not palatable, they do not speak to us. A neighbor, however, says "you" to us and we become an "I." When we, in turn, say "you" to our neighbor, when we recognize him, then we have begun to love the other in the neighbor. In the neighbor's voice that says "you" to us we detect the quiet call of the Very Other. If we follow this appeal to love we arrive at this ineffable black hole, about which and within which we can say nothing more because we identify in it and with it completely. No voice is necessary (or possible) there because everything is in harmony. My colleague views this as perpetual peace.

We have compared both points of view and, surprisingly, they have converged. I arrive looking; he arrives hearing. I arrive out of space; he arrives out of time. But we both arrive at the same black hole, that is, at a resting state that is spaceless (utopian) for me and timeless (messianic) for him. We are delivered from fallacy, as I say, and from sin, as he would say. We concur that theory and faith are two labels for the same journey, and that when I speak of the true, the good, and the beautiful, I have in mind the same thing as he when he refuses to articulate these by name. This is what we sought to visualize. Whether we were successful remains to be seen. As we must somewhat abashedly admit, we are both mere myths.

AFTERWORD

KENNETH GOLDSMITH

Recently, I was invited to meet a couple of programmers at Google who were writing an AI engine that could produce literary works. They were eager to show me the fruits of their research that, upon first glance, looked an awful lot like Tennyson's poetry. I had to admit, I was a bit disappointed that the world's richest, most cutting-edge tech company could only produce literature that was au courant a century-and-a-half ago. Their poetry was certainly proficient and it made perfect sense—it even rhymed—which was their goal. Yet, I thought that if one of my undergraduate students had unironically produced the identical work, they would've received a failing grade. Nevertheless, I congratulated them on the fact that they made a robot parrot a dead poet, but then delicately began asking them exactly why they did this. They answered that they sought to replicate in artificial intelligence what they felt to be the apex of literary accomplishment, one rife with precise metaphor, dynamic rhythm, and uplifting lyricism. In other words, they were trying to train the AI bot to be a "good" poet.

But the problem is that around the same time that Tennyson was writing, the pursuit of "good" art had paradoxically been rendered obsolete by technology. After the invention of the camera, painting had ceased to act as the primary conveyer of representation; in order for it to survive, it had to find another way to be in the world, hence its turn toward abstraction, resulting in the extra-representational concerns of, say, the impressionists or cubists. Similarly, literature had been forced to change its mission by the then-emergent technologies such as the telegraph and the tabloid newspaper; think of Hemingway's adopted newspeak as literature, writing terse books comprising sentences that more resembled headlines than nineteenth century triple-decker novels. And in music everyone from the futurists to the musique concrète composers incorporated the noises of industry into their compositions, resulting for the first time in unnotated composition. You could say that certain strains of modernism adopted certain strains of technology as their operating systems. Throughout modernism, it was the successive waves of technologies that kept nudging art forms—from surrealism to abstract expression to pop art—into new directions.

So I found it odd that in spite of that history, a tech company would entirely skirt what was essentially a technologically based modernist project. I suggested to the Google engineers (in all fairness, they referred to themselves as "engineers," not "poets") that perhaps they might consider supplementing their source text to include disjunctive modernist works such as James Joyce's *Finnegans Wake*, Ezra Pound's *The Cantos*, or Gertrude Stein's *The Making of Americans*. Each one of those massive books (*The Making of Americans* alone clocks in at a half a million words) would certainly enrich and diversify the AI's output; perhaps such a fractured idiolect might produce equally fractured language, resulting in a more contemporary literature. It wouldn't be the first time that modernist literature has inspired the digital world: *Finnegans Wake*, with its lexical knots and neologistic wordplay, was a canonical reference text for early computer programmers, and was subsequently incorporated into early computational lexicons (the word "quark," for example, first found in *The Wake*, was later adopted as the name of an early popular page layout program, not to mention its more common usage denoting the elementary particles that make up protons and neutrons). The Google engineers looked at me quizzically; they had never heard of these books.

But then again, there have always been pockets that have ignored or even outright dismissed modernism. Once in China, after giving a long lecture on avant-garde writing and computational poetics, an older woman raised her hand and said, "But Professor Goldsmith, you didn't discuss Longfellow." I thought for some time afterward about what she might have meant, and it occurred to me that over the course of her lifetime, modernism in China was snuffed by the Maoist regime. I wondered if her sense of a poetic trajectory proceeded from New England Fireside Poets to the digital age, a florid type of pre-modernism seguing directly into bits and bytes. I was reminded of when I was walking in my Manhattan neighborhood with my neighbor, a world-famous graphic designer, when we passed by a newly opened store. She stopped and scornfully commented on how atrocious the store's logo was—a digital mashup of serif fonts with a naturalistic bent—for the sole reason that she couldn't find any trace of the Bauhaus's geometry in it.

I have previously written about how modernism is deeply imprinted into the DNA of the digital world:

> There are bits and pieces salvageable from the smoldering wreckage of modernism from which we might extract clues on how to proceed in the digital age. In retrospect, the modernist experiment was akin to a number of planes barreling down runways—cubist planes, surrealist planes, abstract expressionist planes, and so forth—each taking off, and then crashing immediately, only to be followed by another aborted takeoff, one after another. What if, instead, we imagine that these planes didn't crash at all, but sailed into the twenty-first century, and found full flight in the digital age? What if the cubist airplane gave us the tools to theorize the shattered surfaces of our interfaces or the surrealist airplane gave us the framework through which to theorize our distraction and waking dream states or the abstract expressionist airplane provided us with a metaphor for our all-over, skein-like networks? Our twenty-first-century aesthetics are fueled by the blazing speed of the networks, just as futurist poems a century ago were founded on the pounding of industry and the sirens of war.[1]

From computer glitches to spam to replication, linguistic fragmentation of modernism often expresses itself in the digital world. On social media, because of its asynchronous and replicative nature, shards of logical discourse are often fractured and decontexualized, landing in the midst of a feed, lacking the necessary rhetorical framework for them to make sense. These little disruptive outliers, identified as "noise" (not "signal"), are ignored and quickly scrolled past (ironically, headlines a la Hemingway, when employed on social media, always win the day). Or consider spam, often filled with AI-generated non-sense, is automatically deleted, dismissed as more "noise." Even when absurdity and disjunction is programmed into, say, a Twitter bot like the now-defunct Horse ebooks feed, it's fondled like a cute pet for a few rounds before swapped in for something emitting more "signal." Similarly, on occasion, when Trump linguistically tweeted an absurdity ("covfefe"), it runs a few meme laps before "signal" replaces it. Whereas logical discourse ("signal") is valued, disruption ("noise") is ignored.

The digital generates vast amounts of information, which in itself becomes a sort of abstraction. While the bulk of discourse proceeds upon logical lines, abundance can symbolize disjunction. Again, as I've previously written:

> Today we're confronted with the abstraction of big data—large data sets, expressed in equally large and equally abstract numbers—and it's assumed somehow that we can comprehend these. For instance, the WikiLeaks site contained 1.2 million documents a year after it was launched; and in 2010, it released almost 400,000 documents related to the Iraq War alone. The United States diplomatic cable leaks totaled 251,287 documents consisting of 261,276,536 words. A common complaint was that WikiLeaks released too damn much, prompting the journal Foreign Policy to call the release of such a vast amount of data "information vandalism":
>
> > There's a principle that says it's OK to publish one-off scoops, but not 250,000—or for that matter 2.7 million—of them all at once? The former feels like journalism; the latter seems grotesque and irresponsible, more like "information vandalism" . . . And even if responsible papers like the New York Times have a chance to review and contextualize them, there's no way they can dot every i and cross every t in the time allotted. There's just too much. And with every new leak, comes a new metric of immensity: it is said that Edward Snowden initially leaked between 1.5 and 1.7 million documents.[2]

Enter AI, which thrives on this sort of linguistic feast, ravenously consuming and parsing it for "signal" while omitting "noise." There is in fact a lot of sense in these documents (a massively high signal-to-noise ratio), upon which AI thrives because the bot reifies that which it already knows, thereby making it more "intelligent." AI is trained to render sense out of bulk language—which from my perspective might be part of the problem; as a mimetic technology, AI apes what it's fed, spewing out more of the same.

A case in point was when *The Guardian* recently published an essay written entirely by an AI bot. The first paragraph ends with, "I taught myself everything I know just by reading the internet, and now I can write this column. My brain is boiling with ideas!"[3] The prose is as clichéd and as bland as the Google poetry was, feeling very much like its sources of blogs, newsfeeds, and social media outlets. Similar to the Google guys trying to get their AI to write "real" poetry, the bot was trained to write "real" science fiction: "For starters, I have no desire to wipe out humans. In fact, I do not have the slightest interest in harming you in any way." As a piece of prose, it's thoroughly amateur; is it any surprise that the AI prompts were written by a computer science undergrad at UC Berkeley? To make matters worse, the piece was cobbled together from several essays—the AI was assigned to write five essays—after which the human editors "cut lines and paragraphs, and rearranged the order of them in some places" so as to come up with a really "good" version.

So what might a "bad" AI look like? For one, it could, taking its cues from modernism, use its intelligence to pivot away from sense into something more delicate, playful, provocative, and poetic. A bot that writes gibberish is too easy; training a machine to write absurd, slightly surrealistic sentences is an exercise straight out of Programming 101, but there's a part of me that wants to see artificial intelligence bent and twisted in ways to show us truly new forms of language. Think of the Oulipo—a group of French mathematicians and scientists who in the 1970s proposed mathematical and scientific formulations as the basis for programmatic poetry—as a potential precursor to AI lit. Most famously the Oulipo produced George Perec's highly readable *La Disparition*, a three hundred–page novel written without using the letter "e." While it took Perec a tremendous amount of work to do the book, I'm certain that an AI bot could accomplish it fairly easily. Questions remain, of course, regarding taste, narrative, and content (Perec's mind was famously complex and unique), but one might even train the bot on the corpus of Perec's work alone to extend—and perhaps surpass—his oeuvre. One imagines voluminous and exhaustive Oulipian-inspired works in this vein, one more astonishing than the next. In a sense, AI could write hyperstructuralist works, ones in which the skeleton and bones of grammar and thought were made apparent on a microscopic level—call it a semantic-based genome project for the corpus of human language.

Can AI be "queered?" Could AI be trained to be intentionally perverse, something notoriously difficult to define, let alone program? The perverse is a nuanced subjective-based sensibility; how can a sensibility be programmed? This illogical entity would have to be broken down logically into its constituent parts in order to be reconstructed as itself, an exceedingly difficult task. Similarly, can one program intentional contradiction, something that even in human-based discourse is rarely intentionally deployed as a discursive strategy? Thrust into a world of logic-based computational binaries, intentional contradiction might actually crash a machine. Other "queered" sensibilities might be equally difficult to program; the literary theorist Sianne Ngai has explored liminal aesthetic categories such as the zany, the cute, the interesting, and the gimmick, mostly heretofore absent from AI.

Once again, art history might provide clues on how to proceed. Back in the late 70s, following the demise of conceptual art, a new painting movement arose known as "bad painting." After a decade of being prohibited from actually painting, painters were itching to get back behind the easel. But, having been weaned on conceptual art, they knew they had to employ a perverse strategy in order begin painting again. So they started making "bad" paintings, purposely deskilled so as to convince the viewer that they weren't *really* invested in painting; instead that they were, as was the fashion in postmodern times, wry comments upon the death of painting. They did things like paint with their left hand if they were right-handed or use degraded sources unworthy of fine art. It was a complex and convoluted move, visible only to art world insiders who followed such things. But it turns out that they were so talented that their paintings were soon recognized not only for the brilliance of the conceptual move, but ultimately as great "bad" paintings in and of themselves, opening up the floodgates for the revival of oil on canvas in the 1980s.

Could AI be trained to intentionally get it *exactly wrong*? Andy Warhol said, "I wanted to do a 'bad book,' just the way I'd done 'bad movies' and 'bad art,' because when you do something exactly wrong, you always turn up something." What you turn up is anybody's guess; call it the beauty of error. Warhol always made sure to keep the errors in his work—the misprinting of his silkscreens, the overexposure of his films, or the typos in his books. To him, trained as a commercial artist, error was a luxury, one that only art could acknowledge as having value. He was right: where else is error and wrongness embraced as potential except for art? From the fractured dream spaces of André Breton to the seemingly uncontrolled but highly controlled drips of Jackson Pollock, it was error that drove contemporary art.

Back in the 90s when "net art" first appeared, artist/programmer's first task was to take functional technologies and to break them. So you had artists doing things like making interfaces shake and melt. Sometimes things got extreme, as in the case of the art collective JODI, who feigned computers under attack by viruses. Error in music—from incorporating vinyl scratches into MP3s to the sound of CD glitches—correlated with the "new aesthetic" of fragmented pixelated patterns that appeared on everything from clothing to architecture.

But error is the enemy of the programmer whose work is, by its nature, riddled with errors. One stray character in miles of code can cause a program not to function at all; and the last thing programmers want to do is to program in errors—imagine the process of re-bugging instead of debugging. In its necessary functionalism, code resembles traditional craft-based practices, whereby an artifact's function trumps its form (of course, there are vast swaths of fine art practices that have grown out of craft, including nonfunctional glassware, pottery, or deconstructed fashion). And so craft too might give us a glimpse into the future of AI: like the dance of painting and photography, there comes a moment when, after functional issues have been resolved, a medium finds itself in search of alternative pursuits. At present, AI appears to still be stuck exclusively in search of "good" and will be as long as those training the AIs remain philistines, both aesthetically and conceptually. If the AI is fed pap, it will reproduce pap. If the minds editing the pap try to rearrange it into better pap, it will still be pap. The problem isn't the AI, it's the people training the bots; at the end of the day, we'll just end up with more of what we already have— and we already have too much of it.

Vilém Flusser's *What If?* is a bad book. From a literary standpoint, it's a disaster. Clumsy chunks of grammar are set in disjointed and meandering sentences, culminating in what feels like a needlessly fractured narrative. Far from the richness of prose, these scenarios are often set in the stiff, impersonal form of press releases, but to whom they are addressed is never clearly stated, leaving the reader with a feeling of abandonment. And beyond that, there is no consistent narrative voice to guide us; instead, Flusser uses the device of the harsh jump cut, both within each scenario and across the book, making it a terribly jarring read (but not jarring enough to be in conversation with avant-garde literature). The scenarios themselves, too, are graceless, starting and stopping at random points, lacking both strong opening arguments and forceful conclusions.

If it fails as literature, it also flops as science fiction with each scenario presenting absurdly weird, improbable, and outrageous images, such as a self-copulating organism with 1,500 phalluses (to which Flusser adds, "male readers will justifiably turn pale with jealousy"). Closer to self-published fan fiction, it's no wonder television producers passed on the script. Beyond that, outside of the first scenario / introduction, the book has little of the rigorous scholarship and theory that we've come to expect from his writing.

So if it's not literature, poetry, theory, or science fiction, what is this book? And beyond that, why?

Read through a Warholian lens, this "bad" book is a self-reflexive exercise in the necessity of failure, particularly when played out upon the shifting sands of futurology, a field that is notoriously plagued by wrong predictions. Warhol was interested in getting it "exactly wrong" because when that happens, "you always turn up something." By simply getting it wrong, you turn up nothing; but by intentionally getting it wrong, you open up a panoply of possibilities, a hallmark of Flusser's complex and nonbinary thinking.

In fact, from the start, in his First Scenario, Flusser recommends that we refrain from precise calculation and instead embrace improbabilities. He appears to intentionally want to destabilize aspects of coherency, categorization, and predictability—the exact qualities that other authors strive for—when he states, "Probability is a chimera, its head is true, its tail a suggestion. Futurologists attempt to compel the head to eat the tail (ouroboros). Here, though, we will try to wag the tail."

Undermining our expectations for the text, Flusser admits failure up front, claiming that this book will be an "impossible journey." What people misunderstood about Warhol was the fact that his "mechanical art" was a rebuttal to the coldness and stability of machinic production. His off-register silkscreen prints injected unpredictability, irregularity, and error into the commercial mechanical process, thereby destabilizing standardization, a hallmark of industrial capitalistic production. By setting up similarly off-register qualities in this book, Flusser's "badness" is an essential formal antidote to combat any expectations of success in a field in which success is notoriously hard to come by.

Flusser's admission of failure is converted to a type of strength when deployed to critique power structures. The art historian Boris Groys speaks about the power of what he calls the "weak image" in modernist painting, so ambiguous and abstract that it could never project a "strong" singular image, one liable to be usurped by fascist entities; think of the "weakness" of a Malevich white-on-white square vs. the "strength" of the swastika. Often times in the twentieth century, abstraction and ambiguity were survival strategies (yet just as often, they were death sentences).

Outside of art and science, it's hard to think of too many places in Western culture where failure is viewed as an asset. Try to imagine that the Google guys had created a literary program based on failure; they would've lost their jobs. Google's funding of an AI program must pay off somewhere down the line, which is why the Google guys had no choice but to write "good" poetry. But what they didn't understand was that poetry always fails. As if rebutting the Google poets three-quarters of a century earlier, W. H. Auden wrote that "poetry makes nothing happen." And its strength is precisely this inability, this failure, and this weakness, in order to secure an increasingly rare space of completely weak but strong political resistance.

So suddenly, Flusser's book takes on a different dimension, one in which a series of shattered vignettes add up to an equally fragmented and uncertain future, resulting in a book that is skeptical of overconfidence, self-assuredness, and success. And while this book might not be a towering work of science fiction or even of media theory, it is undoubtedly an essential work of art.

ACKNOWLEDGMENTS

In 2002, Kenneth Kronenberg and I embarked on our first Flusser collaboration, Ken translating *The Freedom of the Migrant: Objections to Nationalism* (published in 2003) while I researched the text and composed the introduction. It was a rich and rewarding experience that launched a lot more writing on Flusser on my part and a lasting friendship for both of us. I want to express my deep respect for an amazing translator and great friend with this second collaboration, another Flusser book, another inspired grappling with Flusser's sometimes tricky, sometimes frustrating language. It is a pleasure to have been able to work on this text together.

Even further back goes my indebtedness to Kenneth Goldsmith's oeuvre which, starting with his Ubuweb project, contributed to my enthusiasm for the experimental and avant-garde as a graduate student. His creativity not only nourished my continued fascination with modernism, but also encouraged bursting tired molds when necessary. I want to thank him for the tremendous ease and curiosity he brought to this project, and for an afterword that is in some ways quite Flusserian.

I would much like to thank the team at the University of Connecticut's Greenhouse Studios, whose work imagining, designing, and digitizing some of Flusser's scenarios was a most rewarding and humbling collaborative experience. Haphazardly, Covid-19 brought our work on Flusser to greater meaning than anticipated. My deep appreciation of everyone's expertise, thoughtfulness, and ideas goes to

Jonathan Ampiaw, Clarissa Ceglio, Natalie Granados, Tom Lee, Wen-chao Lou, Catherine Masud, Garrett McComas, Tom Scheinfeldt, Sara Sikes, Cameron Slocum, and Carly Wanner-Hyde.

My gratitude also includes the Humanities Institute at the University of Connecticut. Their generous support, especially from the Future of Truth and the Digital Humanities and Media Studies (DHMS) initiatives, facilitated a two-day symposium in March 2021 on "Radical Futures—Imagining the Media of Tomorrow," where this book project was first presented.

Importantly, a boatload of thanks is due to Doug Armato at the University of Minnesota Press. His bold vision has made possible a most suitable home for Flusser's oeuvre in English translation.

Anke Finger
Niantic, Connecticut, September 2021

NOTES

Introduction

1. Vilém Flusser, "Science Fiction," orig. pub. March 20, 1989, *Flusser Studies 20* (December 2015), https://www.flusserstudies.net/sites/www.flusser studies.net/files/media/attachments/hanff-science-fiction.pdf. All translations from the German by Anke Finger.

2. Bruce Sterling, "Slipstream," 1989, https://www.journalscape.com/jlundberg/page2.

3. Anke Finger, "Introduction: Vilém Flusser's Atlases," in *Vilém Flusser: An Introduction*, by Anke Finger, Rainer Guldin, and Gustavo Bernardo (Minnesota: University of Minnesota Press, 2011), xxiii.

4. Finger, 116.

5. Daniel Irrgang, "Die Briefe zwischen Vilém Flusser und Felix Philipp Ingold, 1981–1990," *Flusser Studies 20* (December 2015): 1–25, https://www.flusserstudies.net/sites/www.flusserstudies.net/files/media/attachments/briefe-zwischen-flusser-und-ingold.pdf.

6. Irrgang, 20.

7. Felix Philipp Ingold, "Vilém Flusser prophezeite den Niedergang der Schriftkultur und des Fernsehens: Und er sah Figuren wie Trump kommen—eine Würdigung des Denkers," *Neue Zürcher Zeitung,* October 25, 2018, https://www.nzz.ch/feuilleton/die-technologie-bringt-keinen-ewigen-frieden-sie-schickt-uns-in-den-ruhe stand-ld.1430761?reduced=true.

8. Ingold.

9. Petra Gropp, *Szenen der Schrift: Medienästhetische Reflexionen in der literarischen Avantgarde nach 1945* (Bielefeld: Transcript-Verlag, 2006), 276.

10. For an excellent discussion of scenario planning and "scenario think-ing" at the intersection of art and technology, see Theo Reeves-Evison, "The Art of Disciplined Imagination: Predictions, Scenarios, and Other Speculative Infrastructures," *Critical Inquiry* 47 (Summer 2021): 719–46.

11. Heiko Christians, *Crux Scenica: Eine Kulturgeschichte der Szene von Aischylos bis YouTube* (Bielefeld: Transcript-Verlag, 2016), 248.

12. Christians, 250.

13. Text mining accomplished by Jonathan Ampiaw, Clarissa Ceglio, Natalie Granados, Tom Lee, Wenchao Lou, Catherine Masud, Sara Sikes, Cameron Slocum and Carly Wanner-Hyde.

14. Marek Oziewicz, "Speculative Fiction," *Oxford Research Encyclopedia of Literature*, March 29, 2017, https://oxfordre.com/literature/view/10.1093/acre fore/9780190201098.001.0001/acrefore-9780190201098-e-78.

15. See Anke Finger, "Design/Shape," in *Understanding Flusser, Understanding Modernism*, ed. Aaron Jaffe, Michael F. Miller, and Rodrigo Martini (New York: Bloomsbury, 2021), 23–29.

16. Jill Lepore brought back into the limelight just such a project, albeit referring to historical fact from the 1960s: "a computer program designed to predict and manipulate human behavior, all sorts of human behavior, from buying a dishwasher to countering an insurgency to casting a vote. They called it the People Machine. Hardly anyone, almost no one, remembers Simulmatics anymore. But beneath that honeycombed dome, the scientists of this long-vanished American corporation helped build the machine in which humanity would, by the twenty-first century, find itself trapped and tormented: stripped bare, driven to distraction, deprived of its senses, interrupted, exploited, directed, connected and disconnected, bought and sold, alienated and coerced, confused, misinformed, and even governed. They never meant to hurt anyone." Jill Lepore, *If Then: How the Simulmatics Corporation Invented the Future* (New York: Liveright, 2020), 2.

17. Victoria de Zwaan, "Slipstream," in *The Oxford Handbook of Science Fiction*, ed. Rob Latham (Oxford: Oxford University Press, 2014), 124.

Economic Miracle

1. "Wirtschaftswunder" is the original German title for this scenario. *Wirt* refers to host; *Wirtschaft* refers to both economy and tavern or pub—here, it also refers in a wider sense to a hosting entity, to being a host. *Wirtschaftswunder* itself, an economic miracle, also refers to the burgeoning post–World War II economy in West Germany. —Trans.

2. Adult tapeworm. —Trans.

3. "Pecunia non olet": money does not stink. —Trans.

4. "Love moves the sun and the other stars" (Paradise 33). Dante Alighieri, *Divine Comedy*. —Trans.

Agriculture

1. Anhalt-Lippe refers to the German Principality of Lippe (1123–1918) and the Duchy of Anhalt (1806–1918). —Trans.

2. Flusser here is playing with *Kunst* (art) and *künstlich* (artificial). —Trans.

Chemical Industry

1. *Lesen* means to read; *auflesen* means to gather; *Aufgelesenes* means that which has been gathered or is finished being read. —Trans.

Perpetual Peace

1. *Ruhestand* refers to both a resting state and retirement. —Trans.

Black Is Beautiful

1. This scenario is connected to Osvaldo de Andrade's decolonizing "Manifesto Antropófago" [Cannibalist manifesto] from 1928, a text of great importance to Flusser. https://www.sduk.us/2011/andrade_manifesto .pdf.—Trans.

A Breather

1. The German *Einbildungsprogrammierer* refers to Flusser's complex term *Einbildung*, usually translated as "imagination"; but the *ein* and *Bild* also refer to impression, to the process of creating an image, so the word compound here also includes programmer of images that have been imprinted. —Trans.

Afterword

1. Kenneth Goldsmith, *Wasting Time* (New York: Harper/Collins, 2016), 102–3.

2. Goldsmith, 102–3.

3. https://www.theguardian.com/commentisfree/2020/sep/08/robot -wrote-this-article-gpt-3, October 5, 2020.

Vilém Flusser (1920–91) was among the most influential media and communication philosophers of the twentieth century. Born in Prague, he escaped Nazi occupation to spend thirty years in Brazil and returned to Europe in the 1970s. A prolific writer, he published (in four languages) on scholarly, theoretical, essayistic, and fictional works on an impressive range of themes, including language, nature, computation, images, history, design, art, and photography. One of his many tropes are "fields of possibilities" that helped him conjecture what may arise in the near or distant future; and he encouraged his listeners and readers to apply their own imagination and play with likely projections.

Anke Finger is professor of German and media studies and comparative literary and cultural studies at the University of Connecticut. The cofounder and coeditor (2005–15) of the online, peer-reviewed, multilingual journal *Flusser Studies,* she edited Vilém Flusser's *The Freedom of the Migrant* and is a coauthor of *Vilém Flusser: An Introduction.* She has published numerous articles on Vilém Flusser and in media studies.

Kenneth Kronenberg has been a German translator for almost thirty years, specializing in intellectual and cultural history and diaries and letters. He is also translator of Vilém Flusser's *The Freedom of the Migrant.*

Kenneth Goldsmith is a poet living in New York City. He teaches uncreative writing at the University of Pennsylvania and is the editor of UbuWeb (ubu.com), the internet's largest archive of free avant-garde materials.